MOVIE ★ ICON

HEPBU

EDITOR
PAUL DUNCAN

TEXT
F. X. FEENEY

PHOTOS
THE KOBAL COLLECTION

TASCHEN

HONG KONG KÖLN LONDON LOS ANGELES MADRID PARIS TOKYO

CONTENTS

6
AUDREY HEPBURN: INCANDESCENT

by F. X. Feeney

22
VISUAL FILMOGRAPHY

178
CHRONOLOGY

186
FILMOGRAPHY

192
BIBLIOGRAPHY

1

AUDREY HEPBURN: INCANDESCENT

BY F. X. FEENEY

★

AUDREY HEPBURN: EIN SONNENSTRAHL

AUDREY HEPBURN : L'ÉBLOUISSEMENT

AUDREY HEPBURN: INCANDESCENT

by F. X. Feeney

Her beauty has proved timeless – should we be surprised? Equally graceful whether moving or standing still, blessed with a balletic poise, luminous dark eyes and an exquisite profile a Queen might envy, Audrey Hepburn would no doubt have become famous in her youth even if the movies hadn't found her – simply because no self-respecting camera could resist her. What sets her iconic beauty apart now, for us, more than a decade after she quit the stage of this life, is that her physicality is oddly secondary. Her extraordinary good looks merely halo a still-living smile.

She earned that smile the hard way. Born in Brussels, reared in Britain and the Netherlands, she saw bloodshed and starved as a teenager during the worst of World War Two. She also witnessed the Nazi-ordered deportations of defenseless Jews, many her own age or younger. Among these was Dutch girl, Anne Frank, whose diary is now renowned as one of the vital historical documents of that time. Hepburn and Frank had been born a month apart in 1929. In later years, Hepburn was often offered the chance to play Anne but repeatedly turned it down. In the last year of her life, to raise money for UNICEF, Hepburn overthrew her earlier resistance and movingly read from The Diary of Anne Frank at a London concert. When young, however, she felt humbled by her counterpart's true heroism, even shamed (to a healthy degree), because after all, she had survived.

Hepburn instead seized happiness with a keen ferocity. She was a ballerina in her teens, but grew too tall. Her beauty drew on such a cocktail of ancestries – Dutch and Irish, with dashes of Javanese and Hungarian – that upon moving to Britain she quickly caught the eyes

PORTRAIT FOR 'BREAKFAST AT TIFFANY'S' (1961)
Holly Golightly, Truman Capote's madcap heroine and Audrey's most popular role. / Truman Capotes verrückte Heldin Holly Golightly war die populärste Rolle von Audrey Hepburn. / Holly Golightly, l'héroïne farfelue de Truman Capote et le rôle le plus populaire d'Audrey.

"For me, the only things of interest are those linked to the heart."
Audrey Hepburn

of top fashion photographers and filmmakers. By chance, while in Monte Carlo in 1951, she turned the head of the novelist Colette, who took one look and pronounced her "The perfect Gigi."

After that bright moment of discovery, Hepburn found herself the toast not only of Broadway, but Hollywood. Starring role after starring role rushed to her: a princess in *Roman Holiday* (1953); a backyard Cinderella in *Sabrina* (1954); a Russian noble of the Napoleonic era in *War and Peace* (1956); an elfin sprite of high-fashion opposite Fred Astaire in *Funny Face* (1957). Her sweetness was incandescent. In terms of her peak time, the 1950s, Audrey Hepburn was the first of a wave of European beauties (Sophia Loren, Brigitte Bardot, Gina Lollobrigida) who oozed sensuality with an exotic flare that a whole generation of American men felt at home with, having been enchanted by the locals when fighting in Europe only a decade before. With her slim build and adolescent beauty, Hepburn was a trifle less threatening to other women than her more voluptuous contemporaries. If one didn't desire to rescue her, as men lusted to do, one could cheerfully envy her clothes, and great style. For in 1953, Hepburn formed an alliance with designer Hubert de Givenchy that would be lifelong, and globally influential. After John Kennedy became President of the United States in 1961, his wife Jacqueline adopted Givenchy as *her* designer and suddenly the Audrey look was a political force potent enough to melt the frown from Soviet Premier Nikita Khrushchev.

Judged strictly as an actress, Hepburn reaches her full magnitude in *The Nun's Story* (1959) directed by Fred Zinnemann. Her innate intensity perfectly suits that of a young woman who wishes to offer her life up for God – but whose passionate nature also calls her to leave the convent. One can fully believe she is drawn to renounce her vows because she is a deeply practical person, and has a passionate need to *do* good, to actively fight the Nazis and not just meekly accept God's will in the matter. Such a role doubtless played on deep nerves in Hepburn. The conflicts she expresses are profound. So too are the sexy, emotionally pragmatic complexities she brings to life in *Two for the Road* (1966), opposite Albert Finney.

As the *gamine* beauty of her youth faded, Hepburn became a moral presence. She let acting go – life itself took precedence. She devoted herself to raising her sons, Sean and Luca, and as a goodwill Ambassador for UNICEF, bore witness to the ravaged, starving masses of Africa. Her efforts grew so intensive that she eventually skipped medical checkups for herself, and a fatal cancer went undiagnosed.

Her incandescent smile became a gift she gave almost exclusively to hungry children, now. That smile – intense, direct, loving – blazes from what remains of Audrey Hepburn today, in nearly every image, from every phase of her good and giving life.

**PORTRAIT FOR 'BREAKFAST AT TIFFANY'S'
(1961)**
Audrey: "I could never abandon my cat the way Holly does!" / Audrey: „Ich könnte meine Katze nie aussetzen, so wie es Holly tut!" / Audrey : « Je ne pourrais jamais abandonner mon chat comme le fait Holly ! »

AUDREY HEPBURN: EIN SONNENSTRAHL

von F. X. Feeney

Dass sich ihre Schönheit als zeitlos erwies, überrascht kaum. Anmutig in der Ruhe wie auch in der Bewegung, gesegnet mit einer tänzerischen Körperhaltung, leuchtenden dunklen Augen und einem feinen Profil, um das sie manche Königin beneidet – Audrey Hepburn wäre zweifelsohne auch dann berühmt geworden, wenn der Film sie nicht bereits in jungen Jahren entdeckt hätte. Denn kein Fotograf, der etwas auf sich hielt, konnte ihr widerstehen. Über ein Jahrzehnt nach ihrem Abtritt von der Bühne des Lebens zeichnet sich diese Schönheitsikone heute noch dadurch aus, dass das Körperliche merkwürdigerweise zweitrangig war. Ihr außerordentlich gutes Aussehen erscheint als Lichthof eines noch immer lebendigen Lächelns.

Dieses Lächeln hat sie sich hart erarbeitet. In Brüssel geboren, in Großbritannien und den Niederlanden während des Zweiten Weltkriegs aufgewachsen, sah sie Blutvergießen und hungerte als Teenager. Sie wurde Zeuge, als wehrlose Juden auf Geheiß der Nationalsozialisten verschleppt wurden, wobei viele der Opfer in etwa ihr Alter hatten. Unter ihnen war auch ein Mädchen, das aus Deutschland nach Amsterdam geflohen war und dessen Tagebuch heute als bedeutendes Zeitdokument gilt: Anne Frank. Hepburn und Frank waren 1929 im Abstand von nur einem Monat zur Welt gekommen. In späteren Jahren bot man Hepburn des Öfteren an, Anne Frank auf der Bühne zu spielen, doch sie lehnte es immer wieder ab. In ihrem letzten Lebensjahr gab Hepburn den Widerstand auf, um Geld für UNICEF zu sammeln, und las anlässlich eines Londoner Konzerts sehr bewegend aus dem *Tagebuch der Anne Frank*. In jüngeren Jahren hatte sie sich jedoch vom Heldentum ihrer Altersgenossin eher gedemütigt, ja sogar in einem gesunden Maße beschämt gefühlt, weil *sie* ja schließlich überlebt hatte.

Hepburn packte ihr Glück wild entschlossen beim Schopf. Als Teenager hatte sie Ballett getanzt, war dann aber zu sehr in die Höhe geschossen. Ein bunter Reigen an Vorfahren – Niederländer und Iren, Javaner und Ungarn – hatte ihr eine Schönheit beschert, mit der sie nach ihrem Umzug nach Großbritannien sogleich führenden Modefotografen und Filmemachern auffiel. Zufällig

PORTRAIT FOR 'WAR AND PEACE' (1956)
Tolstoy described Natasha as, 'A dark-eyed girl, full of life, with a wide mouth, her bosom undefined.' / Tolstoi beschrieb Natascha als „dunkeläugig, mit einem breiten Mund, nicht hübsch, aber voller Leben". / Tolstoï: « [Natasha est] une fille aux yeux sombres, pleine de vie, avec une large bouche et une poitrine indéfinie. »

„Mich interessieren einzig Dinge des Herzens."
Audrey Hepburn

wurde auch die Romanschriftstellerin Colette 1951 in Monte Carlo auf sie aufmerksam und erklärte sie nach einem einzigen Blick zur „perfekten Gigi".

So wurde Hepburn plötzlich zu einem Broadway- und Hollywood-Liebling. Eine Hauptrolle nach der anderen fiel ihr in den Schoß: eine Prinzessin in *Ein Herz und eine Krone* (1953), ein Hinterhof-Aschenputtel in *Sabrina* (1954), eine russische Adlige in den Napoleonischen Kriegen in *Krieg und Frieden* (1956) und eine Modeelfe an der Seite von Fred Astaire in *Ein süßer Fratz* (1957). Ihr Liebreiz leuchtete ohne fremde Hilfe. Auf ihrem Höhepunkt in den fünfziger Jahren war sie die erste in einer ganzen Folge europäischer Schönheiten (Sophia Loren, Brigitte Bardot, Gina Lollobrigida), die Sinnlichkeit mit einem Hauch Exotik verströmten. Von ihnen fühlte sich eine ganze Generation amerikanischer Männer angezogen, die ein Jahrzehnt zuvor als Soldaten in Europa gewesen waren. Mit ihrer schlanken Figur und ihrer jugendlichen Schönheit erschien Hepburn anderen Frauen etwas weniger bedrohlich als ihre üppiger ausgestatteten Zeitgenossinnen. Wenn man nicht wie die modernen Ritter den Drang verspürte, sie zu retten, dann konnte man sie um ihre Kleider oder ihren Stil beneiden. Denn 1953 ging Hepburn mit dem Modeschöpfer Hubert de Givenchy ein lebenslanges Bündnis ein, das seinen Einfluss rund um den Erdball geltend machte. Nach der Wahl von John F. Kennedy zum Präsidenten der Vereinigten Staaten im Jahr 1961 erkor seine Frau Jacqueline ebenjenen Givenchy auch zu *ihrem* Modeschöpfer. Plötzlich war der Audrey-Look eine politische Kraft, die sogar die Falten auf der Stirn des sowjetischen Regierungschefs Nikita Chruschtschow dahinschmelzen ließ.

Unter rein schauspielerischen Gesichtspunkten erreichte Hepburn ihre volle Blüte in *Geschichte einer Nonne* (1959) unter der Regie von Fred Zinnemann. Die ihr angeborene Intensität passt ausgezeichnet zu einer jungen Frau, die ihr Leben in den Dienst Gottes stellen möchte, aber wegen ihres leidenschaftlichen Naturells das Kloster verlassen muss. Man nimmt ihr ab, dass sie ihr Ordensgelübde widerrufen will, weil sie zutiefst pragmatisch ist und unbedingt Gutes tun will, dass sie die Nazis aktiv bekämpfen und nicht nur sanftmütig den Willen Gottes geschehen lassen möchte. Diese Rolle traf bei Hepburn zweifelsohne einen Nerv. Die Konflikte, die sie zum Ausdruck bringt, sitzen sehr tief. Das gilt auch für die erotische und emotionale Vielschichtigkeit, die sie an der Seite von Albert Finney in *Zwei auf gleichem Weg* (1966) darstellt.

Als die knabenhafte Schönheit ihrer Jugend verblasste, wurde Hepburn zu einer moralischen Größe. Sie gab den Film auf und dafür dem Leben selbst den Vorzug. Sie widmete sich der Erziehung ihrer beiden Söhne Sean und Luca und setzte sich als UNICEF-Botschafterin des guten Willens für die hungernden Massen Afrikas ein. Ihre Anstrengungen nahmen schließlich so viel ihrer Zeit in Anspruch, dass sie die eigene Gesundheitsvorsorge vernachlässigte und eine tödliche Krebserkrankung zu spät erkannt wurde.

Ihr leuchtendes Lächeln war nun fast ausschließlich hungernden Kindern vorbehalten. Dieses intensive, unmittelbare, liebevolle Lächeln strahlte aus allem, was von Audrey Hepburn geblieben ist, aus fast jedem Bild in jeder Phase ihres gutherzigen und großzügigen Lebens.

PORTRAIT FOR 'GREEN MANSIONS' (1959)
As Rima, W. H. Hudson's South American forest
nymph. / Als W. H. Hudsons südamerikanisches
Waldnymphchen Rima. / En Rima, nymphe des bois
sud-américaine créée par W. H. Hudson.

AUDREY HEPBURN : L'ÉBLOUISSEMENT

F. X. Feeney

Sa beauté se révèle éternelle – doit-on s'en étonner ? Aussi gracieuse en mouvement qu'immobile, dotée d'une assurance de ballerine, de lumineux yeux sombres et d'un profil exquis à faire pâlir d'envie une reine, Audrey Hepburn serait sans aucun doute devenue célèbre dans sa jeunesse même si le cinéma ne l'avait pas courtisée – simplement parce qu'aucun objectif digne de ce nom ne pouvait lui résister. Aujourd'hui, plus d'une décennie après son départ de cette scène qu'est la vie, sa beauté idéale se distingue pour nous par le caractère étonnamment secondaire de son physique. Les attraits extraordinaires de sa personne ne font qu'auréoler l'éternel éclat de son sourire.

C'est au prix de maintes épreuves que la jeune Audrey a acquis son sourire. Née à Bruxelles, élevée en Grande-Bretagne et aux Pays-Bas, adolescente pendant les pires années de la Seconde Guerre mondiale, elle connaît les massacres et la famine. Elle est également témoin de la déportation de juifs sans défense, dont beaucoup de son âge, voire plus jeunes. Parmi eux se trouve une petite Néerlandaise, Anne Frank, dont le journal représentera plus tard un des plus précieux documents historiques de cette époque. Hepburn et Anne Frank sont nées à un mois d'écart en 1929. Au cours des années qui suivent, Hepburn a plusieurs fois l'occasion d'interpréter son rôle mais le refuse à chaque fois. La dernière année de sa vie pourtant, afin de lever des fonds pour l'UNICEF, Hepburn met de côté ses réticences et lit avec une grande émotion des passages du Journal d'Anne Frank au cours d'une soirée à Londres. Plus jeune, elle s'était sentie peu de choses à côté de son alter ego héroïque, presque honteuse, simplement parce qu'elle avait survécu.

Hepburn empoigne la vie avec une joie féroce. Danseuse classique à l'adolescence, une croissance trop rapide écourte sa formation. Une fois installée en Grande-Bretagne, sa beauté, qui résulte d'ascendances mêlées – hollandaises et irlandaises – matinées d'une touche javanaise et hongroise, ne tarde pas à attirer l'attention des plus grands réalisateurs et photographes de mode. Par chance, alors qu'elle se trouve à Monte Carlo en 1951, elle fait tourner la tête à la romancière Colette, qui, après un seul regard, décrète qu'elle est « la Parfaite Gigi ».

PORTRAIT (1954)

Her thick eyebrows contradicted fashion but accentuated her beauty. / Ihre starken Augenbrauen entsprachen nicht der Mode, unterstrichen aber ihre Schönheit. / Ses sourcils épais contrariaient la mode mais accentuaient sa beauté.

« Pour moi, les seules choses dignes d'intérêt sont celles du cœur. »
Audrey Hepburn

Après cette révélation éclatante, Hepburn devient la coqueluche de Broadway, mais aussi d'Hollywood. Elle enchaîne les premiers rôles : en princesse dans *Vacances romaines* (1953); en Cendrillon contemporaine dans *Sabrina* (1954); en aristocrate russe sous Napoléon dans *Guerre et Paix* (1956); en sylphide de la mode aux côtés de Fred Astaire dans *Drôle de frimousse* (1957). L'actrice dégage une douceur rayonnante. Lorsqu'elle accède au sommet de la gloire, dans les années 1950, Audrey Hepburn se distingue comme la première représentante de cette constellation de beautés européennes (Sophia Loren, Brigitte Bardot, Gina Lollobrigida) dont la sensualité exotique est familière à toute une génération d'Américains tombée sous le « charme » des femmes du Vieux Continent dix ans plus tôt, tandis qu'ils combattaient l'ennemi allemand. Avec sa silhouette mince et sa beauté adolescente, Hepburn est un tantinet moins menaçante pour les autres femmes que ses contemporaines plus voluptueuses. Et si l'on n'éprouve pas forcément le vif désir de la « sauver », comme en rêve secrètement la gent masculine, on peut bientôt lorgner avec gourmandise sa garde-robe et son extrême élégance. Car en 1953, Hepburn forme avec le couturier Hubert de Givenchy une alliance qui durera toute leur vie et influencera grandement la mode internationale. Une fois John Kennedy devenu président des États-Unis en 1961, son épouse Jacqueline adopte Givenchy comme couturier fétiche et le « look Audrey » devient soudain un instrument politique suffisamment puissant pour dérider Nikita Khrouchtchev.

Sur le strict plan de sa carrière d'actrice, c'est indéniablement dans *Au risque de se perdre* (1959) de Fred Zinnemann que Hepburn atteint toute son ampleur. Son intensité innée convient parfaitement à celle de la jeune héroïne, qui souhaite offrir sa vie à Dieu mais que sa nature passionnée engage aussi à fuir le couvent. Sans doute renonce-t-elle à ses vœux parce qu'elle est avant tout pragmatique et qu'elle ressent l'irrépressible besoin de *faire* le bien, de combattre activement les Nazis au lieu de docilement se résigner à la divine providence. Un tel rôle ne manque pas de faire vibrer les cordes sensibles en elle. Les conflits qu'elle exprime sont profonds. Tout aussi pragmatiques et profondes sont les complexités émotionnelles et frivoles qu'elle incarne dans *Voyage à deux* (1966), avec Albert Finney.

Alors que la beauté *gamine* de sa jeunesse s'estompe, Hepburn devient une instance morale. Elle laisse dériver son métier d'actrice et sa vie revient sur le devant de la scène : elle se consacre à l'éducation de ses fils, Sean et Luca et, en tant qu'Ambassadrice de bonne volonté pour l'UNICEF, elle témoigne des souffrances des peuples décimés et affamés d'Afrique. Ses efforts inlassables la mobilisent tant qu'elle néglige sa propre santé et laisse proliférer un cancer fatal.

Son sourire incandescent était un cadeau qu'elle offrait presque exclusivement à des enfants affamés. Le sourire éblouissant d'Audrey Hepburn rayonne encore aujourd'hui sur chacun de ses clichés, comme à chaque moment de sa vie faite de bonté et de générosité.

PORTRAIT FOR 'FUNNY FACE' (1957)
Wide eyes, long ears, a swan's neck, a photographer's dream. / Große Augen, lange Ohren, Schwanenhals – der Traum eines jeden Fotografen. / De grands yeux, des oreilles allongées, un cou de cygne : le rêve du photographe.

PAGE 22
PORTRAIT (1951)
Looking suitably Roman in this costume test for 'Quo Vadis,' though she wasn't cast in the lead role. / Bei dieser Kostümprobe sieht sie recht römisch aus, aber die Hauptrolle in *Quo Vadis* erhielt sie trotzdem nicht. / Le costume romain lui sied, mais elle n'obtiendra pas le rôle principal dans *Quo Vadis*.

2

VISUAL FILMOGRAPHY

FILMOGRAFIE IN BILDERN
FILMOGRAPHIE EN IMAGES

GIRL

DAS KLEINE MÄDCHEN

LA JEUNE FILLE

"I think sex is overrated."
Audrey Hepburn

„Ich denke, Sex wird überbewertet."
Audrey Hepburn

« Je pense que le sexe est surfait. »
Audrey Hepburn

STILL FROM 'LAUGHTER IN PARADISE' (1951)
Director Mario Zampi took one look and doubled her onscreen time. / Regisseur Mario Zampi warf einen Blick auf sie und verdoppelte sogleich ihre Leinwandzeit. / Le réalisateur Mario Zampi la jaugea d'un seul regard et doubla son temps de présence à l'écran.

PORTRAIT FOR 'LAUGHTER IN PARADISE' (1951)
Noticed right from the start, despite the meager bit parts. / Gleich von Anfang an fiel sie trotz ihrer winzigen Rollen auf. / Remarquée dès ses débuts, malgré des rôles inconséquents.

MARCH 1951

ABC Film Review

STORIES AND PICTURES OF THE FILMS COMING YOUR WAY

4D.

Audrey Hepburn

ASSOCIATED
BRITISH
ARTISTE

IN THIS ISSUE: DAVID LEWIN WRITES "CLOSE-UPS OF THE STARS I KNOW"
OLIVER LANGLEY INTERVIEWS RICHARD ATTENBOROUGH AND SHEILA SIM

PORTRAIT FOR 'LAUGHTER IN PARADISE' (1951)

She'd spent her girlhood training to be a ballerina, but grew too tall. / Als Mädchen hatte sie Ballett getanzt, wurde aber zu groß für eine Ballerina. / Elle a passé son enfance à travailler la danse, mais est vite devenue trop grande pour le ballet.

PORTRAIT (1951)

Despite her sylph-like aura, she was a down to earth lover of children and animals. / Trotz ihrer grazilen Ausstrahlung liebte sie ganz bodenständig Kinder und Tiere. / Malgré son aura de sylphide, elle gardait les pieds sur terre et se laissait attendrir par les enfants et les animaux.

ON THE SET OF 'YOUNG WIVES' TALE' (1951)
"I was his whipping boy," she would later recall of director Henry Cass (center). Nothing she did was good enough, in his opinion, though she got along well with co-stars Nigel Patrick (right) and Joan Greenwood. / „Ich war sein Prügelknabe", erinnerte sie sich später an Regisseur Henry Cass (Mitte). Nichts konnte sie ihm recht machen. Mit ihren Kollegen Nigel Patrick (rechts) und Joan Greenwood verstand sie sich gut. / « J'étais son souffre-douleur", racontera-t-elle plus tard à propos du réalisateur Henry Cass (au centre). Rien de ce qu'elle faisait n'était assez bon à ses yeux, malgré sa bonne entente avec ses partenaires Nigel Patrick (à droite) et Joan Greenwood.

"I decided, very early on, just to accept life unconditionally; I never expected it to do anything special for me, yet I seem to have accomplished far more than I had ever hoped. Most of the time it happened to me without my ever seeking it."
Audrey Hepburn

„Ich entschloss mich schon sehr früh, das Leben ohne Wenn und Aber einfach hinzunehmen. Ich habe nie erwartet, dass es etwas Besonderes für mich bereithält, und doch scheine ich weit mehr erreicht zu haben, als ich mir je erhofft hatte. Meistens geschah es, ohne dass ich je danach gesucht hätte."
Audrey Hepburn

STILL FROM 'YOUNG WIVES' TALE' (1951)
Despite the energy the director spent belittling her,
Audrey Hepburn was the only participant in this film
to receive positive reviews. / Obwohl der Regisseur sie
mit aller Kraft schlechtmachte, war Audrey Hepburn
die einzige an dem Film beteiligte Person, über die
Kritiker Positives schrieben. / Malgré les efforts du
réalisateur pour la rabaisser, Audrey Hepburn est la
seule du générique à recevoir des critiques positives.

« *Très tôt, j'ai décidé d'accepter la vie sans
condition. Je n'ai jamais pensé que cela
m'apporterait quoi que ce soit de spécial et j'ai
pourtant l'impression que ce que j'ai accompli
dépasse toutes mes espérances. La plupart du
temps, les choses sont arrivées sans que je les
provoque.* »
Audrey Hepburn

PAGES 30 & 31
STILLS FROM 'YOUNG WIVES' TALE' (1951)
Beauty aside, the very immediacy and transparent
honesty of her reactions were riveting, whether Nigel
Patrick was coaxing an impromptu laugh (left) or she is
gasping at another's sudden fall (right). / Neben ihrer
Schönheit bestachen die Unmittelbarkeit und
offenkundige Ehrlichkeit ihrer Reaktionen, ob Nigel
Patrick sie zum Lachen brachte (links) oder ob sie
beim Sturz eines anderen erschrak (rechts). /
Sa beauté mise à part, l'immédiateté et la franchise
transparente de ses réactions sont fascinantes, que
Nigel Patrick la fasse soudain rire aux éclats (à gauche)
ou qu'elle reste médusée devant la chute d'un autre
partenaire (à droite).

OPPOSITE TOP
ON THE SET OF 'THE LAVENDER HILL MOB'
(1951)
A bit part as "Chiquita," for director Charles Crichton
(left) opposite Alec Guinness (right). / Eine kleine Rolle
als Chiquita unter der Regie von Charles Crichton
(links) an der Seite von Alec Guinness (rechts). /
Apparition en « Chiquita » pour le réalisateur Charles
Crichton (à gauche) face à Alec Guinness (à droite).

OPPOSITE BOTTOM
ON THE SET OF 'THE LAVENDER HILL MOB'
(1951)
Master cinematographer Douglas Slocombe (left)
assesses the innate radiance. / Douglas Slocombe
(links), ein Altmeister hinter der Kamera, „misst" die
angeborene Ausstrahlung. / Le grand directeur de la
photo Douglas Slocombe (à gauche) mesure son
rayonnement naturel.

STILL FROM 'THE LAVENDER HILL MOB' (1951)
Her line: "Who wants a ciggy?" Everyone found her
impressive. Studio head Michael Balcon later kicked
himself for not signing her to a longtime contract. /
Ihr Text: „Wer will 'ne Lulle?" Alle waren von ihr
beeindruckt. Studiochef Michael Balcon ärgerte sich
später, dass er ihr keinen längerfristigen Vertrag
angeboten hatte. / Sa réplique : « Qui veut une
clope ? » Tout le monde est impressionné. Le chef du
studio, Michael Balcon, se mord les doigts de ne pas
lui avoir fait signer un contrat longue durée.

"I was the tall, thin, shy girl with the big eyes:
But what they wanted to know was whether I could
sing, dance or act, or did I always just stand there
looking in need of a damn good meal?"
Audrey Hepburn

„Ich war das große, dünne, schüchterne
Mädchen mit den großen Augen, aber von mir
wollte man nur wissen, ob ich singen, tanzen
oder schauspielern konnte – oder würde ich nur
herumstehen und so aussehen, als könnte ich
eine verdammt gute Mahlzeit gebrauchen?"
Audrey Hepburn

« J'étais la fille aux grands yeux, grande, mince et
timide : mais ce qu'ils voulaient savoir, c'était si je
savais chanter, danser ou jouer, ou si je me
contentais de rester plantée là comme si je
mendiais un repas. »
Audrey Hepburn

STILL FROM 'THE SECRET PEOPLE' (1952)
Valentina Cortesa (seated, center) spotted Hepburn in
a line of auditioning ballerinas and demanded she be
cast. Cortesa, best remembered for her performance
in 'Thieves' Highway' (1950), warned the budding star
to protect her privacy above all – and Hepburn always
remembered the advice. /
Valentina Cortesa (sitzend, Mitte) entdeckte Hepburn
in einer Schlange Ballerinas, die auf das Vortanzen
warteten, und bestand auf ihr. Cortesa ist
hauptsächlich durch ihre Leistung in *Der Markt der
Diebe* (1950) in Erinnerung geblieben. Sie mahnte den
angehenden Star, vor allem ihre Privatsphäre zu
schützen – und Hepburn hielt sich stets an diesen Rat. /
Valentina Cortesa (assise, au centre) a repéré
Hepburn dans une file de danseuses attendant de
passer une audition et demandé à ce qu'elle soit
choisie pour le rôle. Cortesa, célèbre pour sa
performance dans *Les Bas-fonds de Frisco* (1950),
donna à la vedette en herbe le conseil de protéger sa
vie privée par-dessus tout – et Hepburn ne l'oublia
jamais.

STILL FROM 'THE SECRET PEOPLE' (1952)
The drama centers on a circle of European refugees
bent on assassinating a Balkan diplomat during
Hepburn's performance. / Das Drama handelt von
einem Kreis von Flüchtlingen, die ein Attentat auf
einen Balkan-Diplomaten planen. Es soll stattfinden,
während Nora (Hepburn) auf der Bühne steht. /
Le drame se noue au sein d'un groupe de réfugiés
européens qui prépare l'assassinat d'un diplomate des
Balkans pendant le numéro de danse de Hepburn.

PORTRAIT FOR 'THE SECRET PEOPLE' (1952)
The role of a ballerina fit her lightly and easily. /
Die Rolle einer Ballerina fiel ihr ausgesprochen
leicht. / Elle endosse avec légèreté et facilité ce rôle
de ballerine.

AUDREY HEPBURN & COLETTE
The great novelist saw Hepburn at the beach
and declared, "Voilà ma Gigi!" / Die große
Romanschriftstellerin sah Hepburn am Strand und rief:
„Voilà ma Gigi!" / La grande romancière vit Hepburn
sur la plage et s'écria : « Voilà ma "Gigi" ! »

*"You've worked hard all your life. I have faith
that all that work is about to pay off now - for both
of us."*
Colette

*„Du hast dein ganzes Leben lang hart gearbeitet.
Ich glaube fest daran, dass sich all diese Arbeit
jetzt auszahlt - für uns beide."*
Colette

STILL FROM 'GIGI' (1951)
Anita Loos, who adapted the novel for the stage,
noted of Colette's young discovery, "Whatever she
did, she stood out." / Anita Loos, die die
Bühnenfassung des Romans geschrieben hatte, meinte
über Colettes Entdeckung: „Sie hob sich bei allem,
was sie tat, von der Menge ab." / Anita Loos, qui
adapta le roman au théâtre, déclara à propos de la
jeune découverte de Colette : « Quoi qu'elle fît, elle
sortait du lot. »

*« Tu as travaillé dur toute ta vie. Je suis convaincue
que tout ce travail est sur le point de payer - pour
nous deux. »*
Colette

STILL FROM 'ROMAN HOLIDAY' (1953)
"The real star of the picture is Audrey Hepburn,"
Peck shrewdly declared before the picture opened. /
„Der wirkliche Star dieses Films ist Audrey Hepburn",
erklärte Peck geschickterweise vor dem Filmstart. /
« La vraie vedette du film, c'est Audrey Hepburn »,
déclara Peck, perspicace, avant la présentation
du film.

ON THE SET OF 'ROMAN HOLIDAY' (1953)
Gregory Peck was so impressed by Hepburn's
screen test that he insisted her billing equal his
own. / Gregory Peck war von Hepburns Kameratest so
beeindruckt, dass sie auf seinen Wunsch neben ihm
über dem Filmtitel genannt wurde. / Gregory Peck fut
si impressionné par les essais de Hepburn qu'il exigea
qu'elle partage la tête d'affiche avec lui.

ON THE SET OF 'ROMAN HOLIDAY' (1953)
Director William Wyler rehearses the scene where the
runaway Princess (Hepburn) finds herself the platonic
houseguest of ambitious reporter Peck. / Regisseur
William Wyler probt eine Szene, in der sich die
Ausreißerprinzessin (Hepburn) als platonischer Gast
des ehrgeizigen Reporters Bradley (Peck) wieder-
findet. / Le réalisateur William Wyler répète la scène
où la Princesse en fuite (Hepburn) se retrouve l'hôte
platonique de l'ambitieux reporter interprété par
Peck.

PAGES 44/45
ON THE SET OF 'ROMAN HOLIDAY' (1953)
Between takes (and bites of ice cream) with Peck and
Wyler. / Mit Peck und Wyler zwischen Einstellungen
und Eiscreme. / Entre deux prises (et deux bouchées
de glace), avec Peck et Wyler.

PORTRAIT FOR 'ROMAN HOLIDAY' (1953)
Blacklisted writer Dalton Trumbo scripted this tale of
a 'Cinderella in reverse' using another writer as a
front. / Drehbuchautor Dalton Trumbo, der auf der
schwarzen Liste stand, schrieb diese „umgekehrte"
Aschenputtelgeschichte unter dem Namen eines
Strohmanns. / L'écrivain Dalton Trumbo, inscrit sur
la liste noire, livra le scénario de ce « Cendrillon
à rebours » mais le fit signer par John Dighton.

STILL FROM 'ROMAN HOLIDAY' (1953)
Inevitably, the young runaway Princess shakes the
reporter's cynicism while stealing a brief taste of
spontaneous romance outside her royal duties. / Die
junge Prinzessin auf Abwegen kann den Zynismus des
Reporters erschüttern und lässt sich außerplanmäßig
auf eine spontane Romanze ein. / Forcément, la jeune
Princesse en fuite ébranle le cynisme du reporter et
vole quelques instants de romance spontanée à son
emploi du temps royal.

*"Here was a girl good at everything but shedding
tears... When it came to a poignant scene, Wyler
had to scare the wits out of her."*
Gregory Peck

*„Hier war also ein Mädchen, das alles konnte, nur
keine Tränen vergießen ... Wenn eine rührende
Szene anstand, musste Wyler sie zu Tode
erschrecken."*
Gregory Peck

STILL FROM 'ROMAN HOLIDAY' (1953)
Despite their shared happiness, love is not to be.
She must return to her life of royal obligation. / Trotz
des gemeinsamen Glücks ist ihre Liebe nicht von
Dauer: Sie muss zu ihrem Leben und ihren Pflichten
als Prinzessin zurückkehren. / Malgré leur bonheur
partagé, leur amour est impossible. Elle doit retourner
aux obligations de son rang.

*« Voilà une fille qui savait tout faire sauf verser des
larmes... Au moment des scènes poignantes, Wyler
était obligé de lui faire une peur bleue. »*
Gregory Peck

STILL FROM 'ROMAN HOLIDAY' (1953)
The Princess reassumes her regal identity. Hepburn
was a sensation the instant the film opened, in August,
1953, winning covers of 'Time' and 'Life', and an Oscar
the following spring. / Die Prinzessin schlüpft wieder
in ihre königliche Rolle. Sofort nach dem Filmstart im
August 1953 war Hepburn in aller Munde. Sie kam auf
die Titelseiten von *Time* und *Life* und erhielt im
folgenden Frühjahr einen Oscar. / La Princesse
reprend son identité régalienne. Dès le lancement du
film, en août 1953, Hepburn fait sensation : elle fait la
couverture des magazines *Time* et *Life* et remporte
un oscar le printemps suivant.

*"After so many drive-in waitresses becoming movie
stars... along comes class. ... In that league there's
only ever been Greta Garbo, the other Hepburn,
and maybe Ingrid Bergman. It's a rare quality, but
boy, do you know when you've found it."*
William Wyler

*„Nachdem so viele Kellnerinnen aus Drive-in-
Restaurants Filmstars geworden waren, ... kam nun
endlich [jemand mit] Klasse ... In dieser Liga gab es
überhaupt nur Greta Garbo, die andere Hepburn
und vielleicht Ingrid Bergman. Es ist eine seltene
Eigenschaft, aber, Junge, wenn man sie findet,
dann weiß man's!"*
William Wyler

ON THE SET OF 'ROMAN HOLIDAY' (1953)

Wyler, ever the perfectionist, guides her through the motions. John F. Kennedy told a reporter that 'Roman Holiday' was his favorite movie of all time, and Audrey Hepburn his favorite actress. / Der ewige Perfektionist Wyler zeigt ihr, was sie zu tun hat. John F. Kennedy vertraute einem Reporter an, dass *Ein Herz und eine Krone* sein Lieblingsfilm und Audrey Hepburn seine Lieblingsschauspielerin sei. / Wyler, toujours perfectionniste, guide ses mouvements. John F. Kennedy a déclaré à un journaliste que *Vacances romaines* était son film préféré et Audrey Hepburn son actrice favorite.

« *Après toutes ces serveuses de drive-in devenues vedettes de cinéma… enfin, la classe. […] Dans cette catégorie, il n'y aura toujours que Greta Garbo, l'autre Hepburn et peut-être Ingrid Bergman. C'est une qualité rare, mais bon Dieu! Quand vous l'avez trouvée, vous le savez tout de suite.* »
William Wyler

GROWING PAINS

★

WACHSTUMSSCHMERZEN

LA DOULOUREUSE MATURITÉ

STILL FROM 'SABRINA' (1954)
A lovesick witness to the fairytale lives of others, she
toys with suicide using fumes from the car exhausts. /
Liebeskrank spielt sie mit dem Gedanken, sich mit
Autoabgasen das Leben zu nehmen. / Amoureuse
éconduite, elle songe à mettre fin à ses jours en
inhalant des gaz d'échappement.

PAGES 54/55
PORTRAIT FOR 'SABRINA' (1954)
Hepburn and William Holden briefly became lovers
during the shoot. / Hepburn und William Holden
waren während der Dreharbeiten kurze Zeit liiert. /
Hepburn et William Holden ont une brève liaison
pendant le tournage.

PAGE 50
STILL FROM 'SABRINA' (1954)
Washing a car in style, as her chauffeur father stands
by. / Autowäsche mit Stil. Ihr Vater, der Chauffeur,
schaut zu. / Lavant une voiture avec style, sous le
regard du chauffeur.

ON THE SET OF 'SABRINA' (1954)
Her self-destructive fantasies now spent, Sabrina
ponders what to do. / Nachdem sie ihre Selbst-
mordfantasien überwunden hat, überlegt sie nun, was
sie als nächstes tun soll. / Ses fantasmes d'auto-
destruction balayés, Sabrina réfléchit à ce qu'elle va
faire.

STILL FROM 'SABRINA' (1954)
Cary Grant was director Billy Wilder's first choice for the role – and Humphrey Bogart knew it. / Cary Grant war Billy Wilders erste Wahl für die Rolle – und Humphrey Bogart wusste es. / Cary Grant était le premier choix du réalisateur Billy Wilder pour le rôle, et Humphrey Bogart le savait.

ON THE SET OF 'SABRINA' (1954)
Checking her make-up before stepping aboard a landlocked sailboat for close-ups with Humphrey Bogart. / Hier überprüft sie ihre Maske, bevor sie ein trockengelegtes Segelboot für Nahaufnahmen mit Humphrey Bogart besteigt. / Vérification du maquillage avant de monter à bord d'un voilier de décor pour des plans rapprochés avec Humphrey Bogart.

PAGES 58 & 59
ON THE SET OF 'SABRINA' (1954)
Wilder had once made a living ballroom dancing, and loved to show off his prowess. / Wilder hatte früher seinen Lebensunterhalt als Eintänzer verdient. / Wilder avait jadis gagné sa vie comme danseur de salon et il adorait faire admirer ses prouesses.

STILL FROM 'SABRINA' (1954)
"I was terrified of Bogart, and he knew it," she would later laugh. He responded kindly, behind a mask of rough joviality. / „Ich hatte eine Heidenangst vor Bogart, und er wusste es", lachte sie später. / « Bogart me terrifiait et il le savait bien », se souviendra-t-elle en riant.

ON THE SET OF 'SABRINA' (1954)
As Bogart said, "Audrey's like a good tennis player – unpredictable – she varies her shots." / „Audrey ist wie eine gute Tennisspielerin. Sie ist unberechenbar – jeder Schlag, jede Einstellung ist anders", sagte Bogart von Audrey. / Bogart : « Audrey est comme un bon joueur de tennis – imprévisible, elle varie ses coups. »

PORTRAIT FOR 'WAR AND PEACE' (1956)
"I'm strong as a horse," said Hepburn in the broiling heat of a Roman summer. / „Ich bin stark wie ein Pferd", sagte Hepburn in der brütenden römischen Hitze. / « Je suis solide comme un cheval », lança Hepburn lors d'un tournage dans la chaleur toride d'un été romain.

PORTRAIT FOR 'WAR AND PEACE' (1956)
Mel Ferrer is well cast as Prince Andrei, Audrey ideal as Natasha, and Henry Fonda fatally miscast as Pierre. / Mel Ferrer gab einen guten Prinzen Andrej ab, Audrey ist die ideale Natascha und Henry Fonda als Pierre eine totale Fehlbesetzung. / Mel Ferrer est parfait en Prince Andreï, Audrey idéale dans le rôle de Natasha et Henry Fonda une erreur de casting en Pierre.

PAGES 64 & 65: 'WAR AND PEACE' (1956)
Audrey rehearses (left), then recreates (right) a festive American dance step described by Tolstoy. / Audrey probt einen von Tolstoi beschriebenen Tanzschritt. / Tolstoï décrit un entraînant pas de danse américain. Audrey commence par s'entraîner avec ardeur, pour finir par le réinventer.

STILL FROM 'WAR AND PEACE' (1956)
"His eyes simply penetrated me," she would later say, of falling in love with Ferrer. He took charge of her career in ways that irritated others, but made her best work possible. / „Seine Augen haben mich einfach durchbohrt" – so erklärte sie später, wie sie sich in Ferrer verliebte. Seine Art, sich ihrer Karriere anzunehmen, irritierte zwar, ermöglichte aber ihre besten Leistungen. / « Ses yeux me transperçaient », confiera-t-elle plus tard à propos de son coup de foudre pour Ferrer. Il prit en main sa carrière d'une manière qui en irrita certains, mais sut tirer d'elle le meilleur.

STILL FROM 'WAR AND PEACE' (1956)
As Natasha, living through Napoleon's invasion of Russia in 1812, Hepburn gives life to extremes of girlish joy and mature grief. / Natascha erlebt im Jahre 1812 Napoleons Überfall auf Russland mit. In dieser Rolle verkörperte Hepburn die Extreme von mädchenhafter Unbeschwertheit und reifer Trauer. / En Natasha, pendant l'invasion de la Russie par Napoléon en 1812, Hepburn interprète des sentiments extrêmes allant de la joie enfantine au deuil adulte.

STILL FROM 'LOVE IN THE AFTERNOON' (1957)
Again under the direction of Billy Wilder, and once
again – as in 'Sabrina' – paired with a much older star in
a role intended for the ever-elusive Cary Grant.
Hepburn nevertheless hit it off well with the kind,
unpretentious Gary Cooper. / Wieder unter der Regie
von Billy Wilder und wieder – wie in *Sabrina* – an der
Seite eines viel älteren Stars. Für dessen Rolle war
ursprünglich der schwer fassbare Cary Grant
vorgesehen. Hepburn verstand sich aber sehr gut mit
dem freundlichen, bescheidenen Gary Cooper. / Une
nouvelle fois sous la direction de Billy Wilder, et

encore – comme pour *Sabrina* – appariée à une
vedette masculine bien plus âgée dans un rôle créé
pour l'insaisissable Cary Grant. Hepburn s'entend très
bien avec le généreux et modeste Gary Cooper.

STILL FROM 'LOVE IN THE AFTERNOON' (1957)
As the daughter of a private detective, Audrey becomes intrigued by the casefile of womaniser Cooper. She creates a false past for herself, cobbled together from her father's investigations, and uses it to tease and intrigue Cooper. He bites. / Als Tochter eines Privatdetektivs ist Audrey Hepburn fasziniert vom Fall des Frauenhelden Flannagan (Cooper). Aus den Akten ihres Vaters bastelt sie sich eine erfundene Lebensgeschichte zusammen und versucht, Flannagans Aufmerksamkeit zu gewinnen. Er beißt an. / Audrey, qui joue la fille d'un détective privé, est intriguée par le dossier de l'homme à femmes interprété par Cooper. Elle s'invente un passé à partir du résultat des investigations de son père et l'utilise pour attirer Cooper dans ses filets. Il finit par mordre à l'hameçon.

"Off camera, she was just an actress. She was very thin, a good person, sometimes standing on the set she disappeared. But [when she stood before the cameras] there was something... just absolutely adorable about her. You trusted her."
Billy Wilder

« Hors caméra, elle n'était qu'une actrice. C'était quelqu'un de bien, parfois sa mince silhouette passait inaperçue sur le plateau. Mais [face à la caméra] elle avait simplement quelque chose... d'absolument exquis. Elle inspirait la confiance. »
Billy Wilder

„Wenn die Kamera nicht lief, war sie nur eine Schauspielerin. Sie war sehr dünn, ein guter Mensch, und manchmal fiel sie kaum auf, wenn sie am Set stand. Aber [vor der Kamera] hatte sie etwas ... einfach vollkommen Entzückendes an sich. Man konnte sich auf sie verlassen."
Billy Wilder

PAGES 72 & 73
ON THE SET OF 'LOVE IN THE AFTERNOON' (1957)
Ariane demonstrates a bit of bullfighting technique, with a lean loaf of French bread as a sword, and a breadbasket for a hat. Stylist Grazia De Rossi (later briefly visible in 'The Nun's Story') helps her check her look in a mirror. / Ariane führt die Technik des Stierkampfs vor - mit einem Baguette als Schwert und einem Brotkorb als Hut. Ihre Friseuse Grazia De Rossi, die später kurz in Geschichte einer Nonne zu sehen ist, hilft ihr, im Spiegel das Aussehen zu überprüfen. / Ariane fait une démonstration de technique tauromachique avec une longue baguette en guise de sabre. La styliste Grazia De Rossi (que l'on aperçoit dans Au risque de se perdre) l'aide à contrôler les détails dans le miroir.

ON THE SET OF 'LOVE IN THE AFTERNOON' (1957)
Director Billy Wilder (dark glasses, at right) guides his stars to the place of their impending picnic - one of the key scenes of the film. / Regisseur Billy Wilder (mit dunkler Brille, rechts) führt seine Stars an die Stelle, an der ihr Picknick stattfinden soll - eine der Schlüsselszenen des Films. / Le réalisateur Billy Wilder (lunettes noires, à droite) guide ses vedettes jusqu'à l'endroit où ils vont pique-niquer - une des scènes clés du film.

PAGES 74 & 75
ON THE SET OF 'LOVE IN THE AFTERNOON' (1957)
Her balletic turn as a toreador continues for Cooper, then pauses for an adjustment from Wilder. / Der tänzerische Auftritt als Stierkämpferin wird für Cooper fortgesetzt, bis Wilder ihn unterbricht, um etwas zu korrigieren. / Son numéro chorégraphié de matador continue pour Cooper, puis s'interrompt pour laisser Wilder y apporter une amélioration.

ON THE SET OF 'LOVE IN THE AFTERNOON' (1957)

Billy Wilder, rehearsing Cooper and Hepburn in a bit of romantic slapstick when a lost shoe delays what might have been a stormy goodbye. / Billy Wilder probt mit Cooper und Hepburn eine romantische Slapstickeinlage, bei der ein verlorener Schuh einen ansonsten stürmischen Abschied verzögert. / Billy Wilder, faisant répéter à Cooper et Hepburn une scène d'un romantisme « tarte à la crème » dans laquelle une chaussure égarée retarde ce qui aurait pu être un adieu houleux.

"Titism has taken over the country. [Audrey Hepburn] may singlehanded make bosoms a thing of the past. Never again will the director have to invent shots where the girl leans forward for a scotch and soda."
Billy Wilder

„Das ,Tittentum' hat dieses Land voll im Griff. [Audrey Hepburn] schafft es möglicherweise im Alleingang, dass Busen der Vergangenheit angehören. Nie wieder werden Regisseure Einstellungen erfinden müssen, in denen sich eine Frau für einen Scotch mit Soda vorbeugt."
Billy Wilder

STILL FROM 'LOVE IN THE AFTERNOON'
(1957)
A final goodbye is foiled as Ariane hurries alongside
the train, and her lover refuses to let her go. / Ein
letztes Lebewohl wird vereitelt, als Ariane neben dem
Zug herläuft und ihr Liebhaber sie nicht gehen lassen
will. / L'ultime adieu est lui aussi contrecarré alors
qu'Ariane court le long du train et que son amant
refuse de la laisser partir.

« Le culte du néné a envahi le pays. [Audrey
Hepburn] peut d'un revers de main envoyer les
grosses poitrines au grenier. Plus jamais un
réalisateur ne devra inventer des plans où la fille se
penche en avant pour prendre un scotch ou un
soda. »
Billy Wilder

PAGES 78 & 79
ON THE SET OF 'FUNNY FACE' (1957)
Yet another May-December romance, this time with
a stylish American photographer, in Paris. Here, Jo
(Hepburn, left) poses in the red glare of her man's
darkroom. / Schon wieder eine Romanze zwischen
Lenz und Lebensabend, diesmal mit einem schicken
amerikanischen Fotografen in Paris. Hier posiert Jo
(Hepburn, links) im Rotlicht in der Dunkelkammer
ihres Liebhabers. / Encore une romance d'été, cette
fois à Paris, avec un photographe américain branché.
Ici, Jo (Hepburn à gauche) pose sous la lumière rouge
dans la chambre noire de son bien-aimé.

STILL FROM 'FUNNY FACE' (1957)
Fred Astaire is the cameraman, closely modeled (in terms of style) on fashion great Richard Avedon, who assisted with the production, creating memorable 'freeze frame' montages. / Fred Astaire, der Mann hinter der Kamera, wurde (stilistisch) dem Vorbild des großen Modefotografen Richard Avedon nachempfunden. Letzterer steuerte denkwürdige Standfotomontagen zu dem Film bei. / Fred Astaire joue le photographe ; il s'inspire largement (stylistiquement parlant) du géant de la photo de mode Richard Avedon – consultant sur le film –, lequel participe à la création de mémorables séquences avec incrustation d'images figées.

"Audrey was always entirely certain of who she was and how she wanted us to see her."
Richard Avedon

„Audrey war sich stets vollkommen sicher, wer sie war und wie sie von uns gesehen werden wollte.“
Richard Avedon

« Audrey était toujours totalement certaine de ce qu'elle était et de la manière dont elle voulait que nous la voyions. »
Richard Avedon

STILL FROM 'FUNNY FACE' (1957)
With Kay Thompson and Fred Astaire, atop the Eiffel
Tower. Despite the up-to-date surface, Astaire had
starred in the Broadway stage version of 'Funny Face'
in 1928, opposite his sister Adele / Mit Kay Thompson
und Fred Astaire auf dem Eiffelturm. Trotz der
aktualisierten Oberfläche ist die Vorlage älter: Bereits
1928 hatte Astaire in dem Musical *Funny Face* – der
Musicalfassung von *Ein süßer Fratz* – neben seiner
Schwester Adele am Broadway auf der Bühne
gestanden. / Avec Kay Thompson et Fred Astaire,
au sommet de la tour Eiffel. Malgré l'actualité de
l'histoire, Astaire avait déjà joué une version plus
ancienne de *Drôle de frimousse* : la comédie musicale
Funny Face (sur la scène de Broadway en 1928, avec sa
sœur Adele).

PAGES 82 & 83
PORTRAITS FOR 'FUNNY FACE' (1957)
Hepburn's character Jo wears the all-black outfit of
the Empathicalists, a satirical take on the
Existentialists. / Hepburns Figur Jo trägt das schwarze
Outfit der Empathikalisten, eine Parodie auf die
Existentialisten. / Le personnage incarné par Hepburn
arbore la tenue noire des grands maîtres
empathicalistes dans une parodie de l'existentialisme.

STILL FROM 'FUNNY FACE' (1957)
Her white socks are a particularly brilliant visual touch, suggested by director Stanley Donen. / Die weißen Socken setzen einen genialen optischen Akzent und gehen zurück auf einen Vorschlag von Regisseur Stanley Donen. / Ses socquettes blanches constituent une touche visuelle particulièrement brillante, suggérée par le réalisateur Stanley Donen.

STILL FROM 'FUNNY FACE' (1957)
Jo performs her piece 'Basal Metabolism'– a jitterbug jazz ballet whose very title is a witty spoof on the abstract, interpretive titles that stalk modern dance. / Jo führt das Jitterbug-Jazz-Ballett „Basal Metabolism" auf – schon allein der Titel parodiert auf witzige Weise die abstrakten, bedeutungsvoll einherstolzierenden Namen moderner Tanzstücke. / Jo interprète *Basal Metabolism*, un « Jitterbug » jazzy dont le titre parodie les titres conceptuels typiques de la danse moderne.

ON THE SET OF 'FUNNY FACE' (1957)
During the day, Jo (Hepburn, red coat, back to us) ascends the fashion world as a top model for 'Quality Magazine.' / Tagsüber ist Jo (Hepburn, im roten Mantel, mit dem Rücken zur Kamera) Topmodel für *Quality Magazine* und macht sich in der Modewelt einen Namen. / Pendant la journée, Jo (Hepburn, en manteau rouge, de dos) se fait un nom dans le monde de la mode comme mannequin vedette pour *Quality Magazine.*

"She seemed to have a line drawn around her, the way only children have. Whatever she did, she stood out."
Anita Loos

„Es schien, als ob eine Linie um sie gezogen wäre, wie sonst nur bei Kindern. Sie hob sich bei allem, was sie tat, von der Menge ab.“
Anita Loos

STILL FROM 'FUNNY FACE' (1957)
Sweeping down a staircase as 'winged victory.' "It was just good luck I did it once and didn't break my leg." /
Als „geflügelte Siegesgöttin" schwebt sie die Treppe herab. „Es war reines Glück, dass ich es nur einmal tun musste und mir dabei nicht die Beine brach." /
Dévalant un escalier comme une « victoire ailée ».
« J'ai vraiment eu de la chance de n'avoir à le faire qu'une fois et de ne pas m'être cassé la jambe. »

« C'était comme si une ligne avait été dessinée autour d'elle, ce que l'on ne connaît que chez les enfants. Quoiqu'elle fît, elle sortait du lot. »
Anita Loos

STILL FROM 'FUNNY FACE' (1957)
Receiving a note from Astaire, as Jo prepares for yet
another photo shoot. / Während sich Jo auf ein
weiteres Fotoshooting vorbereitet, erhält sie eine
Nachricht von Dick (Astaire). / Jo reçoit un mot
d'Astaire alors qu'elle se prépare pour une nouvelle
séance photo.

PAGES 90/91
STILL FROM 'FUNNY FACE' (1957)
The wedding of model and maestro. Despite her
training, Hepburn worried she was no match for
Astaire as a dance partner. / Die Hochzeit des Models
mit dem Maestro. Trotz ihrer Ausbildung befürchtete
Hepburn, Astaire tänzerisch nicht gewachsen zu sein. /
Le mariage du modèle et du maître. Malgré son travail,
Hepburn craignait de ne pas être une partenaire de
danse digne d'Astaire.

STILL FROM 'FUNNY FACE' (1957)
Richard Avedon's fashion photos were often praised as
"frozen dances," an effect director Donen worked
carefully with the photographer to replicate. / Richard
Avedons Modefotos wurden häufig als „erstarrte
Tänze" gepriesen. Regisseur Donen arbeitete eng mit
dem Fotografen zusammen, um diesen Effekt
nachzuahmen. / Les photos de mode de Richard
Avedon, qualifiées de « danses figées », ont inspiré le
réalisateur Stanley Donen.

TRANSFORMATIONS

★

WANDLUNGEN

TRANSFORMATIONS

ON THE SET OF 'GREEN MANSIONS' (1959)
Half Cuban-American, half-Irish, Mel Ferrer was her
husband for 15 years. / Mel Ferrer, Amerikaner
kubanisch-irischer Herkunft, war 15 Jahre lang mit ihr
verheiratet. / Moitié Américano-cubain, moitié
Irlandais, Mel Ferrer restera son époux pendant 15 ans.

PAGE 92
PORTRAIT FOR 'THE NUN'S STORY' (1959)
As Sister Luke, closely modeled on the real-life nun,
Marie-Louise Habets. / Die Figur von Schwester Luke
ist eng an die Nonne Marie-Louise Habets angelehnt. /
Dans le rôle de Sœur Luke, qui s'inspire d'une nonne
bien réelle, Marie-Louise Habets.

PORTRAIT FOR 'GREEN MANSIONS' (1959)
As 'Rima, the bird-girl,' the angelic protector of
animals in the South American forest. / Als „Rima,
das Vogelmädchen" spielt sie den Schutzengel der
Tiere im südamerikanischen Urwald. / En « Rima,
la femme-oiseau », ange gardien des animaux de
la forêt amazonienne.

LOVE SCENES TO REMEMBER

This beautiful portrait is the first of a series of scenes from the year's films we think that you will not want to forget.

Audrey Hepburn as Rima and Anthony Perkins as Abel, the unforgettable lovers in "Green Mansions" (M.-G.-M.)

PORTRAIT FOR 'GREEN MANSIONS' (1959)
Anthony Perkins as Abel, a cynical adventurer smitten by Rima's goodness. / Anthony Perkins als der zynische Abenteurer Abel, der von Rimas Güte hingerissen ist. / Anthony Perkins est Abel, un aventurier cynique terrassé par la bonté de Rima.

PUBLICITY FOR 'GREEN MANSIONS' (1959)
Hepburn was at the height of her early fame, and the film was much-anticipated. / Hepburn hatte den Gipfel ihres frühen Ruhms erreicht, und der Film wurde mit großer Spannung erwartet. / Hepburn est au sommet de sa gloire précoce et le film est très attendu.

STILL FROM 'GREEN MANSIONS' (1959)
Hunters and tribesmen, outraged by Rima's
interference on the animal kingdom's behalf, hunt her
instead. Ferrer recreated the Amazonian rain forest on
25 acres of MGM soundstage, using over 250 tons of
props – trees, plants, bark canoes – imported from
South America. / Jäger und Stammesangehörige sind
empört über Rimas Engagement für die Tierwelt und
jagen sie. Ferrer baute den Amazonasregenwald in
einer zehn Hektar großen MGM-Studiohalle nach und
verwendete dabei mehr als 250 Tonnen Requisiten.
Pflanzen und Einbäume ließ er eigens aus Südamerika
importieren. / Chasseurs et autochtones, indignés
par l'ingérence de Rima au nom du règne animal,
la prennent en chasse. Ferrer recréa la forêt
amazonienne en studio sur 13 hectares appartenant
à la MGM et y fit dresser plus de 250 tonnes de
décors – arbres, végétation, canoës – importés
d'Amérique du Sud.

*"I need a lot of loving, being loved and giving love.
Love does not terrify me, but the going-away of it
does."*
Audrey Hepburn

*„Ich brauche sehr viel Liebe – ich will geliebt
werden und Liebe schenken. Liebe ängstigt mich
nicht, aber ihr Verlust schon."*
Audrey Hepburn

*« J'ai besoin de beaucoup d'amour – d'être aimée et
de donner de l'amour. L'amour ne me terrifie pas,
mais sa disparition, si. »*
Audrey Hepburn

STILL FROM 'GREEN MANSIONS' (1959)
Abel, fleeing a civil war in his native Caracas, is saved
by Rima from a venemous snakebite, and though they
become lovers, he is unable to save her. / Rima rettet
Abel das Leben, der auf der Flucht vor dem
Bürgerkrieg im heimischen Caracas von einer
Giftschlange gebissen wurde. Obwohl sie ein
Liebespaar werden, kann er sie nicht retten. / Abel,
fuyant la guerre civile qui ravage sa Caracas natale, est
sauvé de la morsure mortelle d'un serpent par Rima,
et bien qu'ils deviennent amants, il ne parvient pas à
la sauver.

STILL FROM 'THE NUN'S STORY' (1959)
Taking her vows. The nun about to cut her hair (with tray, at left) is Grazia De Rossi, Hepburn's actual hairdresser. / Die Nonne legt die Profess ab. Die Ordensschwester, die ihre Haare abschneidet (links, mit Tablett), wird gespielt von Hepburns Friseuse Grazia De Rossi. / Prononçant ses vœux. La nonne qui s'apprête à lui couper les cheveux (avec le plateau, à gauche) est Grazia De Rossi, la vraie coiffeuse d'Hepburn.

PORTRAIT FOR 'THE NUN'S STORY' (1959)
On location in the Congo, where she endured the heat in good cheer. "I didn't swelter," she said later. "All that covering keeps the heat out." / Bei den Dreharbeiten im Kongo ertrug sie die Hitze mit großer Gelassenheit. „Mir war nicht besonders warm", sagte sie später. „Die dicken Gewänder hielten die Hitze draußen." / En tournage au Congo, où elle subit la chaleur avec bonne humeur. « Je n'ai pas étouffé de chaleur », confiera-t-elle plus tard. « Toutes ces couches de vêtements empêchent la chaleur de pénétrer. »

*"If I am not for myself, who will be for me? And if
I am for myself alone, what am I?"*
Sister Luke (Audrey Hepburn), 'The Nun's Story' (1959)

„Wenn ich nicht für mich selbst bin, wer wird dann
für mich sein? Und wenn ich allein für mich bin, was
bin ich dann?"
Sister Luke (Audrey Hepburn), *Geschichte einer Nonne*
(1959)

« Si je ne vis pas pour moi, qui le fera à ma place ? Et
si je ne vis que pour moi, que suis-je ? »
Sister Luke (Audrey Hepburn), *Au risque de se perdre* (1959)

STILL FROM 'THE NUN'S STORY' (1959)
"He is a genius," Sister Luke is warned, of the sexy Dr
Fortunati (Peter Finch). "He is also a bachelor and an
unbeliever. Don't ever think for an instant your habit
will protect you." / „Er ist ein Genie", wird Schwester
Luke vor dem erotischen Dr. Fortunati (Peter Finch)
gewarnt. „ ... Denkt nicht einen Augenblick lang, dass
euch eure Tracht schützt." / « C'est un génie » : voilà
Sœur Luke avertie contre le séduisant Dr Fortunati
(Peter Finch). « [...] Ne croyez surtout pas que votre
habit vous protège. »

STILL FROM 'THE NUN'S STORY' (1959)
When Sister Luke shows mercy to a mental patient,
she is beaten within an inch of her life. Here she
directs he be subdued with compassion. / Ihre
Barmherzigkeit gegenüber einem Geisteskranken
bezahlt Schwester Luke beinahe mit dem Leben.
Hier gibt sie Anweisungen, dass man ihn rücksichtsvoll
bändigen soll. / Lorsque Sœur Luke fait preuve de
clémence à l'égard d'un malade, elle manque le payer
de sa vie. Elle demande ici à ce qu'il soit maté avec
compassion.

STILL FROM 'THE UNFORGIVEN' (1960)
Audrey plays Rachel Zachary, a young Native American woman raised as a white, in this adaptation of a novel by Alan Le May (author of 'The Searchers'). Co-star and producer Burt Lancaster ordered director John Huston to steer the film away from the themes of racism and instead make "a swashbuckler." Huston grudingly complied, to his everlasting regret. / Audrey spielt die junge Indianerin Rachel Zachary, die als Weiße erzogen wurde. Es handelt sich um die Verfilmung eines Romans von Alan Le May, dem Autor von *Der Schwarze Falke*. Kollege und Produzent Burt Lancaster wies Regisseur John Huston an, das Thema Rassismus im Film zu meiden und stattdessen einen reinen Abenteuerfilm zu drehen. Huston gab

widerwillig nach, was er später bereute. / Audrey joue Rachel Zachary, une jeune Indienne d'Amérique élevée comme une blanche, dans cette adaptation du roman d'Alan Le May (l'auteur de *La Prisonnière du désert*). Son partenaire et producteur Burt Lancaster avait demandé au réalisateur John Huston de s'écarter du thème du racisme et d'adopter un style « cape et épée ». Huston s'etait plié à sa volonté de mauvaise grâce, à son éternel regret.

"Alert, full of the ardor of an explorer, with nothing of the lassitude or languor of such voluptuous and earthbound sex goddesses as Elizabeth Taylor and Ingrid Bergman, or the over-eager Marilyn Monroe."
Molly Haskell

„Aufgeweckt, voller Entdeckungslust, ganz ohne die Trägheit und das Schmachten solch üppiger, erdgebundener Sexgöttinnen wie Elizabeth Taylor und Ingrid Bergman oder die übereifrige Marilyn Monroe."
Molly Haskell

STILL FROM 'THE UNFORGIVEN' (1960)
The zeal with which Hepburn commits herself to the role is one of the resulting film's few abiding virtues. / Der Eifer, mit dem sich Hepburn in die Rolle stürzte, ist einer der wenigen Pluspunkte des Films. / Le zèle typique avec lequel Hepburn se dévoue à son rôle confère au film une de ses rares qualités.

« Alerte, pleine d'une ardeur d'exploratrice, si loin de la lassitude ou de la langueur de déesses sensuelles, voluptueuses et terrestres comme Elizabeth Taylor et Ingrid Bergman, ou de l'excès de zèle de Marilyn Monroe. »
Molly Haskell

STILL FROM 'THE UNFORGIVEN' (1960)
Rachel faces her true heritage. Audrey also had troubles – during the production she was thrown by a horse and miscarried. / Rachel sieht sich mit ihrer wahren Herkunft konfrontiert. Bei den Dreharbeiten erlebte Audrey Hepburn eine schwierige Zeit: Sie wurde vom Pferd geworfen und erlitt eine Fehlgeburt. / Rachel affronte sa véritable origine. Audrey subit aussi des épreuves : au cours du tournage, une chute de cheval lui fait perdre l'enfant qu'elle porte.

STILL FROM 'THE UNFORGIVEN' (1960)
Pleading with brother Burt Lancaster, with whom she has always been a little bit in love – openly so, now that both discover they are not related by blood. / Sie fleht ihren Bruder (Burt Lancaster) an, in den sie immer ein wenig verliebt war. Nun, da beide festgestellt haben, dass sie nicht blutsverwandt sind, können sie ihre Liebe offen zeigen. / Elle supplie son frère (Burt Lancaster) pour lequel elle a toujours éprouvé un amour qu'elle peut désormais révéler au grand jour, puisqu'ils savent tous deux qu'ils ne partagent pas le même sang.

STILL FROM 'BREAKFAST AT TIFFANY'S' (1961)
Holly Golightly, Truman Capote's archetypal sex
kitten, was a deliberate stretch for Hepburn, and her
proudest: "The best thing I've ever done," she would
later confide to friends, "because it was the
hardest." / Für die Rolle des archetypischen
Sexkätzchens Holly Golightly musste sich Hepburn
anstrengen, aber sie war stolz darauf: „Das war meine
beste Leistung", vertraute sie später Freunden an,
„weil es die schwierigste war." / Holly Golightly,
archétype de la minette de Truman Capote, est un
rôle à contre-emploi pour Hepburn. Elle en est
consciente, et très fière : « La meilleure chose que
j'aie jamais faite », confia-t-elle à des amis, « parce que
ç'a été la plus difficile. »

STILL FROM 'BREAKFAST AT TIFFANY'S' (1961)
After a night of partying, Holly Golightly delightedly
eyes the wealth of the world on her way home. / Nach
einer durchfeierten Nacht bekommt Holly Golightly
auf dem Weg nach Hause glänzende Augen angesichts
des Reichtums, der ihr aus der Auslage
entgegenfunkelt. / Après une nuit de fête, Holly
Golightly rentre chez elle en contemplant avec délice
les merveilles qu'offre le monde.

STILL FROM 'BREAKFAST AT TIFFANY'S'
(1961)
Truman Capote was bitter: "Marilyn Monroe wanted the part so badly that she worked up two whole scenes all by herself to play for me. She was terrifically good. Then Paramount double-crossed me and cast Audrey." / Truman Capote war verärgert: „Marilyn Monroe war so versessen auf die Rolle, dass sie zwei ganze Szenen alleine ausarbeitete, um sie mir vorzuspielen. Sie war ungeheuer gut. Dann hat mich Paramount übers Ohr gehauen und Audrey genommen." / Truman Capote était amer : « Marilyn Monroe voulait tellement le rôle qu'elle avait répété toute seule deux scènes entières pour me les montrer. Elle était incroyablement bonne. Et puis je me suis fait doubler par la Paramount, qui a engagé Audrey. »

STILL FROM 'BREAKFAST AT TIFFANY'S' (1961)
Hepburn took it in her stride that the novelist preferred a different star, then committed herself with her usual wholehearted aplomb. The irony, given these offscreen conflicts, is that it is now impossible to read the book without seeing Audrey Hepburn. / Hepburn nahm es gelassen, dass der Romanautor einen anderen Star vorzog, und widmete sich ihrer Arbeit mit gewohnter Selbstsicherheit. / Hepburn prit avec sérénité le fait que le romancier ait préféré une autre vedette, puis s'engagea dans le rôle avec son aplomb et sa passion habituels.

"Money never made anyone happy in and of itself, but it always gave me a real sense of security, so it enhanced my ability to be happy."
Audrey Hepburn

„Geld hat an und für sich noch nie jemanden glücklich gemacht, aber es hat mir stets ein Gefühl der Sicherheit gegeben und auf diese Weise meine Fähigkeit zum Glücklichsein gesteigert."
Audrey Hepburn

« L'argent en lui-même n'a jamais rendu personne heureux, mais il m'a toujours donné un vrai sentiment de sécurité, ce qui a renforcé ma capacité à être heureuse. »
Audrey Hepburn

STILL FROM 'BREAKFAST AT TIFFANY'S' (1961)
A hit song came out of the film, 'Moon River,' melody by Henry Mancini, lyrics by Johnny Mercer. Both men felt directly inspired by the spirit of mysterious, invincible optimism Hepburn so freely projected, even at her loneliest. / Aus dem Film stammt der Hit „Moon River" mit Musik von Henry Mancini und Text von Johnny Mercer. Beide Männer inspirierte unmittelbar der geheimnisvolle, unerschütterliche Optimismus, den Hepburns Holly Golightly selbst in ihren einsamsten Stunden ausstrahlt. / Le film donne naissance à *Moon River*, la chanson à succès composée par Henry Mancini sur des paroles de Johnny Mercer. Les deux auteurs se sont directement inspirés de l'optimisme mystérieux et invincible que projetait si librement Hepburn, même dans les mauvais jours.

STILL FROM 'BREAKFAST AT TIFFANY'S' (1961)
Married Patricia Neal leaves money and a kiss for her
toyboy novelist George Peppard. Holly understands
the situation. / Eine verheiratete Frau (Patricia Neal)
hinterlässt Geld und einen Kuss für ihren Gespielen,
den Romanschriftsteller Paul (George Peppard). Holly
versteht die Situation. / Patricia Neal, une femme
mariée, laisse de l'argent et un baiser pour son
souffre-douleur, le romancier interprété par George
Peppard. Holly comprend la situation.

"She had that rare thing – audience authority.
The thing that makes everybody look at you when
you're onstage."
Raymond Rouleau

„Sie besaß dieses seltene Etwas – Autorität beim
Publikum, diese Eigenschaft, die alle Blicke auf
dich lenkt, wenn du auf der Bühne stehst."
Raymond Rouleau

« Elle possédait cette chose rare : la présence.
La chose qui fait que tous les regards se portent
sur vous lorsque vous êtes en scène. »
Raymond Rouleau

STILL FROM 'BREAKFAST AT TIFFANY'S' (1961)
Holly, feeling fragile, just wants to be held. George
Peppard is a macho variant of the androgynous
narrator of Capote's novel. / Holly fühlt sich nicht gut
und möchte nur festgehalten werden. George
Peppard spielt eine Machovariante des androgynen
Erzählers in Capotes Roman. / Fragilisée, Holly veut
seulement qu'on la prenne dans les bras. George
Peppard est une variante machiste du narrateur
androgyne du roman de Capote.

"She has authentic charm. Most people simply
have nice manners."
Alfred Lunt

„Sie besitzt echten Charme. Die meisten Menschen
haben einfach nur eine nette Art."
Alfred Lunt

« Elle a un charme authentique. La plupart des
gens se contentent d'avoir de jolies manières. »
Alfred Lunt

STILL FROM 'BREAKFAST AT TIFFANY'S' (1961)
Holly's cat, called "Cat", is her familiar, for Holly has a touch of the sorceress – but more deeply, it is her double. / Hollys Kater Cat ist ihr Vertrauter, denn Holly besitzt etwas Hexenhaftes – eigentlich ist er jedoch ihr Doppelgänger, ein unabhängiger Streuner, der immer wieder auf den Füßen landet. / Le chat de Holly – « Le Chat » –, est son démon intime, car Holly a quelque chose d'une sorcière – mais il est aussi, plus profondément, son double, un nomade indépandant, toujours capable de retomber sur ses pattes.

STILL FROM 'BREAKFAST AT TIFFANY'S' (1961)
Here, Holly suffers one of her periodic rages and hurls
a Teddy Bear at Peppard, as if to say, "Here's all you
ever were to me." / Hier bekommt Holly einen ihrer
gelegentlichen Anfälle und wirft einen Teddybären
nach Paul (Peppard), als wolle sie ihm sagen: „Das ist
alles, was du mir je bedeutet hast." / Ici, Holly traverse
une de ses crises de rage chroniques et jette un ours
en peluche au visage de Peppard, comme pour lui dire
« Voilà tout ce que tu as jamais été pour moi. »

STILL FROM 'BREAKFAST AT TIFFANY'S' (1961)
When Peppard sells a story, he and Holly celebrate by
doing things they had never done before. She buys
something at Tiffany's ... /
Als Paul (Peppard) eine seiner Geschichten verkauft,
feiert er mit Holly: Sie tun Dinge, die sie vorher noch
nie gemacht haben. Sie kauft etwas bei Tiffany's ... /
Peppard fête son succès avec Holly. Ils décident de
faire des choses qu'ils n'ont jamais faites avant. Elle
achète quelque chose chez Tiffany's ...

STILL FROM 'BREAKFAST AT TIFFANY'S' (1961)
... he steals from a store. These actions strengthen
their relationship. /
... während er einen Ladendiebstahl begeht. Die
beiden Taten festigen ihre Beziehung. /
... tandis que lui vole dans un magasin. Ces gestes
renforcent leur relation.

STILL FROM 'BREAKFAST AT TIFFANY'S' (1961)
Holly, having run afoul of a local crime lord, must flee
the country and leave her cat – and a great piece of
her heart – behind her. / Holly, die einem Gangster-
boss in die Quere gekommen ist, muss die Stadt
fluchtartig verlassen. Sie lässt ihren Kater zurück –
und ein großes Stück ihres Herzens. / Holly, qui a des
ennuis avec un caïd local, doit quitter le pays et
abandonner son chat – avec un gros morceau de son
cœur – derrière elle.

*"Sex appeal is something you feel deep down
inside. I can convey as much fully clothed, picking
apples off a tree or standing in the rain."*
Audrey Hepburn

*„Sex-Appeal ist etwas, was man tief im Inneren
spürt. Ich kann ihn ebenso gut voll bekleidet
rüberbringen, beim Äpfelpflücken oder wenn ich im
Regen stehe."*
Audrey Hepburn

STILL FROM 'THE CHILDREN'S HOUR' (1962)
The tragic irony is that this rumor awakens MacLaine's
character to deep feelings of attraction to Hepburn
that she had otherwise refused to acknowledge, even
to herself – and this is all the more painful for her
friend. / Die tragische Ironie liegt darin, dass das
Gerücht tiefe Gefühle für Karen an den Tag bringt, die
Martha nie eingestehen wollte, nicht einmal sich
selbst – für ihre Freundin wird es dadurch noch
schmerzlicher. / Ironie tragique : cette rumeur éveille
en Martha une attirance profonde à l'égard d'Hepburn,
des sentiments qu'elle avait jusque-là refusé de
s'avouer – ce qui est d'autant plus douloureux pour
son amie.

STILL FROM 'THE CHILDREN'S HOUR' (1962)
Lillian Hellman's superb play was still considered too
volatile for the screen, at least by director William
Wyler, and so alas he was at pains to water it down as
much as he could. / Lillian Hellmans herausragendes
Bühnenstück galt als noch zu brisant fürs Kino –
jedenfalls meinte das Regisseur William Wyler. Er tat
sein Möglichstes, den Stoff zu verwässern. /
La magnifique pièce de Lillian Hellman était encore
jugée trop explosive pour le grand écran, en tout cas
par le réalisateur William Wyler, qui fit donc, hélas,
tout son possible pour l'édulcorer.

PAGES 126/127
STILL FROM 'CHARADE' (1963)
In this Hitchcock-like adventure, George Kennedy is
eager to avenge a double-cross with his new metal
mitts. / In diesem Abenteuer à la Hitchcock will sich
Scobie (George Kennedy) mit seiner neuen
Metallklaue dafür rächen, dass er hereingelegt
wurde. / Dans cette aventure à la Hitchcock, George
Kennedy est impatient de se venger d'une trahison en
se servant de ses nouvelles pinces.

STILL FROM 'THE CHILDREN'S HOUR' (1962)
Wounded to her heart that her fiancee has rejected
her because he can't get the rumor out of his head. /
Karen ist tief getroffen, als ihr Verlobter sie
zurückweist, weil er das Gerücht nicht verdrängen
kann. / Blessée que son fiancé la rejette parce qu'il ne
parvient pas à s'ôter la rumeur de l'esprit.

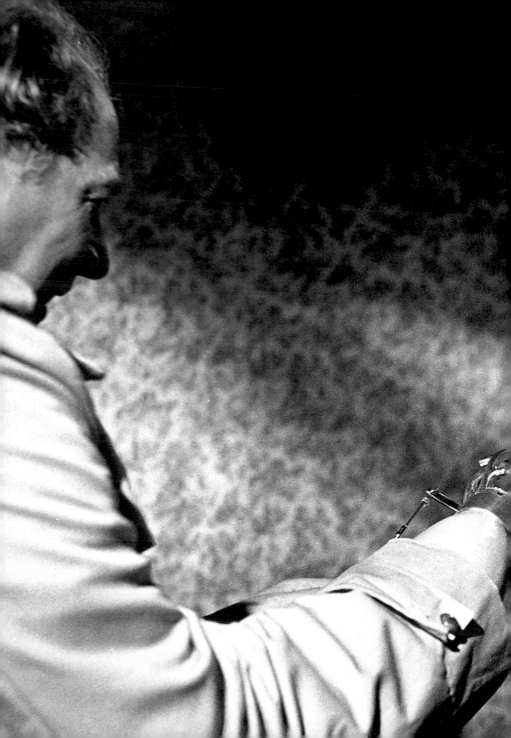

STILL FROM 'CHARADE' (1963)
The game of double, triple and quadruple cross has
Hepburn dodging the otherwise alluring entreaties of
the Mystery Man played by Cary Grant. / Durch ihr
Doppelspiel auf mehreren Ebenen entzieht sich
Reggie (Hepburn) immer wieder dem ansonsten recht
verführerischen geheimnisvollen Fremden (Cary
Grant). / Le jeu des trahisons en cascade pousse
Hepburn à se dérober aux instances pourtant
séduisantes de l'homme mystérieux interprété par
Cary Grant.

STILL FROM 'CHARADE' (1963)
Our heroine conceals herself on the Paris
metro. / Die Heldin versteckt sich in der Pariser
Metro. / Notre héroïne se cache dans le métro
parisien.

STILL FROM 'CHARADE' (1963)
Walter Matthau is a seemingly reliable official on this merry-go-round, but almost nobody is who they seem. / Bartholomew (Walter Matthau) tritt in diesem Karussell als zuverlässiger Beamter auf, doch in dem Film ist fast niemand, was er scheint. / Walter Matthau semble être un responsable digne de confiance, mais, dans ce manège, presque personne n'est ce qu'il paraît.

STILL FROM 'CHARADE' (1963)
Of all the older men Hepburn was paired with, only Cary Grant (wincing here, as she applies salve to his wounds) was her equal in agelessly sexy humor, and vigor. / Von allen älteren Filmpartnern war ihr nur Cary Grant in Sachen Vitalität und Humor ebenbürtig – alterslos und sexy. / De tous les hommes plus âgés avec lesquels Hepburn a été associée, seul Cary Grant fut son égal en humour, en vitalité et en sex-appeal intemporel.

ON THE SET OF 'PARIS WHEN IT SIZZLES' (1964)
Again, Paris – her primary residence in Hollywood
films – reunited with William Holden under the
direction of Richard Quine (right). / Wieder in Paris –
ihrem ersten Wohnsitz in Hollywood-Filmen – und
wieder an der Seite von William Holden, aber diesmal
unter der Regie von Richard Quine (rechts). / Paris,
encore – son principal lieu de résidence dans les films
hollywoodiens –, et de nouveau avec William Holden
sous la direction de Richard Quine (à droite).

STILL FROM 'PARIS WHEN IT SIZZLES' (1964)
Holden, recalling their affair during 'Sabrina,' called
Hepburn "The love of my life." They remained the
dearest of friends. / Holden nannte Hepburn „die
Liebe meines Lebens", als er sich an ihre Affäre
während der Dreharbeiten zu *Sabrina* erinnerte.
Sie blieben stets eng befreundet. / Holden disait
d'Hepburn, évoquant leur liaison sur le tournage de
Sabrina, qu'elle avait été l'« amour de [sa] vie ». Ils sont
restés des amis très proches.

STILL FROM 'PARIS WHEN IT SIZZLES' (1964)
George Axelrod's playful screenplay centers on a
Hollywood writer (Holden) desperate to deliver a
script in three days – so he engages a temp (Hepburn),
to whom he can dictate it. The resulting interplay
weaves wild fantasies with everyday reality, wherein
the writer becomes a fallen knight (left) and the
doe-eyed secretary enjoys an utterly gratuitous but
welcome bubble-bath (right). Kneeling at right:
director Richard Quine. / Das spielerische Drehbuch
von George Axelrod handelt von einem Hollywood-
Autor (Holden), der in drei Tagen ein Drehbuch
abliefern muss und eine Aushilfssekretärin (Hepburn)
für das Diktat engagiert. In der Folge vermischen
sich wilde Fantasien mit der Alltagswirklichkeit:
Der Schriftsteller wird zum gefallenen Ritter (links),
während seine rehäugige Sekretärin völlig grundlos ein
höchst willkommenes Schaumbad nimmt (rechts).

Rechts kniet Regisseur Richard Quine. / Le scénario
enjoué de George Axelrod tourne autour d'un auteur
hollywoodien (Holden) qui, n'ayant plus que trois jours
pour rendre un scénario, engage une intérimaire
(Hepburn) à qui le dictor. L'interaction entre les deux
personnages débouche sur un mélange de fantasme et
de réalité quotidienne, dans lequel l'auteur devient un
chevalier déchu (à gauche) et la secrétaire aux yeux de
biche s'offre le luxe d'un bon bain moussant (à droite).
Agenouillé à droite, le réalisateur Richard Quine.

ON THE SET OF 'PARIS WHEN IT SIZZLES'
(1964)

STILL FROM 'PARIS WHEN IT SIZZLES' (1964)
Writer and Muse play a game of hide and seek with
the idea hiding primarily within his head, though she is
happy to help him search for it. / Der Schriftsteller
und seine Muse spielen Verstecken: Die Ideen
versteckt er hauptsächlich in seinem Kopf, aber Gaby
hilft ihm gerne bei der Suche. / L'auteur et sa muse
partent en quête de l'idée qu'il avait en tête au départ,
et elle prend plaisir à l'aider.

„Ich bekam überhaupt nicht mit, dass da zwischen
Audrey Hepburn und William Holden was im Busch
war. Ich bin mir immer noch nicht sicher."
Billy Wilder

"I was completely unaware that anything was
going on between Audrey Hepburn and William
Holden. I'm still not sure."
Billy Wilder

« J'ignorais totalement qu'il se passait quelque
chose entre Audrey Hepburn et William Holden.
Je ne suis toujours sûr de rien, d'ailleurs. »
Billy Wilder

**ON THE SET OF 'PARIS WHEN IT SIZZLES'
(1964)**
Hepburn and Holden have fun on the set. / Hepburn
und Holden haben bei den Dreharbeiten ihren Spaß. /
Hepburn et Holden s'amusent sur le plateau.

"She was the love of my life."
William Holden

„Sie war die Liebe meines Lebens."
William Holden

« Elle a été l'amour de ma vie. »
William Holden

STILL FROM 'MY FAIR LADY' (1964)
As Eliza Doolittle, George Bernard Shaw's fiery, highly
perfectible flower girl, chatting with her chimney-
sweep father (Stanley Holloway). / Als George
Bernard Shaws Eliza Doolittle. Das temperamentvolle
und in hohem Maße nachhilfebedürftige Blumen-
mädchen plaudert mit seinem Vater, dem Schornstein-
feger Alfred (Stanley Holloway). / Dans le rôle d'Eliza
Doolittle, la bouquetière turbulente et sans manières –
imaginée par George Bernard Shaw dans son roman
Pygmalion –, en discussion avec son père (Stanley
Holloway), ramoneur de son état.

STILL FROM 'MY FAIR LADY' (1964)
Hepburn worked extra hard to strengthen her singing
voice, and master a cockney accent, for this early,
dirt-poor phase in Eliza's journey. / Zu Beginn ihres
langen Wegs zählt Eliza zu den Ärmsten der Armen.
Für diesen Abschnitt arbeitete Hepburn sehr hart an
ihrer Singstimme und am Cockney-Akzent. / Hepburn
travaille sans relâche pour renforcer sa voix et
maîtriser l'accent cockney avant de jouer cette
première étape miséreuse de la vie d'Eliza.

STILL FROM 'MY FAIR LADY' (1964)
Henry Higgins (Rex Harrison, center), a smug specialist
in phonetics, delights at the prospect of transforming
rough-edged Eliza into a lady of quality, through a trick
of diction. / Der selbstgefällige Phonetikprofessor
Henry Higgins (Rex Harrison, Mitte) findet großes
Vergnügen an der Herausforderung, die ungeschlif-
fene Eliza in eine Lady mit guter Aussprache und
Ausdrucksweise zu verwandeln. / Henry Higgins (Rex
Harrison, au centre), professeur de phonétique
prétentieux, jubile à l'idée de transformer l'Eliza mal
dégrossie en dame de qualité par un simple travail de
diction.

ON THE SET OF 'MY FAIR LADY' (1964)
Harrison and Hepburn listen to director George Cukor. / Harrison und Hepburn hören Regisseur George Cukor zu. / Harrison et Hepburn écoutent le réalisateur George Cukor.

"There are actresses who will do an enormous number of takes and don't mind... Audrey Hepburn never minded – she rather liked it."
George Cukor

„Einige Schauspielerinnen benötigen eine enorme Zahl an Takes, ohne dass es ihnen was ausmacht ... Audrey Hepburn machte es nie was aus – ihr gefiel es sogar."
George Cukor

« Il est des actrices qui tournent une énorme quantité de prises sans que cela ne les dérange... Cela ne dérangeait jamais Audrey Hepburn – elle aimait plutôt ça. »
George Cukor

STILL FROM 'MY FAIR LADY' (1964)
Higgins and his crony, Colonel Pickering (Wilfrid
Hyde-White, right) exult at their first triumph in
reforming Eliza, bursting into the classic song 'The Rain
in Spain.' / Higgins und sein alter Freund Colonel
Pickering (Wilfrid Hyde-White, rechts) frohlocken
angesichts ihres ersten Triumphs mit Eliza und singen
den Klassiker „Es grünt so grün". / Higgins et son vieil
ami le colonel Pickering (Wilfrid Hyde-White, à droite)
exultent après leur premier triomphe de Pygmalions
– ils ont réussi à transformer Eliza ! – en entonnant la
célèbre chanson The Rain in Spain.

STILL FROM 'MY FAIR LADY' (1964)
Before she can lucidly state that "the rain in Spain falls mainly on the plain," Eliza's pronunciation is triple- and quarduple-checked by the professor's proliferating gadgets. / Bis sie klar ausdrücken kann, was geschieht, „wenn Spaniens Blüten blüh'n", muss sich Eliza eingehenden Untersuchungen mit den zahllosen Gerätschaften des Professors unterziehen. / Avant qu'elle puisse affirmer sans frémir qu'« un chasseur sachant chasser doit savoir chasser sans son chien », la diction d'Eliza est vérifiée et corrigée grâce aux multiples gadgets du professeur.

PAGES 144/145
STILL FROM 'MY FAIR LADY' (1964)
A triumphant dance / Ein triumphierender Tanz. / La danse du triomphe.

PORTRAIT FOR 'MY FAIR LADY' (1964)
Cecil Beaton's spectacular clothing designs might have
swallowed any lesser beauty. In matters of style,
Hepburn is never outdone, or upstaged. / Cecil
Beatons aufsehenerregende Kostüme hätten eine
andere Frau leicht in den Hintergrund treten lassen,
doch in Sachen Stil lässt sich Hepburn von nichts und
niemandem ausstechen. / Les costumes spectacu-
laires créés par Cecil Beaton auraient pu ensevelir une
beauté moindre. En matière de style, Hepburn ne peut
être ni surpassée, ni éclipsée.

STILL FROM 'MY FAIR LADY' (1964)
The old Eliza bursts out at the racetrack: "C'mon,
Dover, move yer bloomin' arse!" / Die alte Eliza platzt
auf der Rennbahn mit dem Ausruf heraus: „Na los,
Dover, sonst streu ich dir Pfeffer in 'n Arsch!" / L'Eliza
d'avant refait irruption sur un champ de courses : « Eh,
Fleur Bleue, magne-toi le cul ! »

STILL FROM 'MY FAIR LADY' (1964)
Meeting, and suitably deceiving, royalty. / Sie trifft auf
den Adel – und kann ihn täuschen. / Rencontre royale
... avec duperie à la clé.

PORTRAIT FOR 'MY FAIR LADY' (1964)
Posing for Cecil Beaton, toward whom director Cukor
began to feel jealously competitive. / Sie posiert für
Cecil Beaton, auf den Regisseur Cukor immer
eifersüchtiger wurde. / Posant pour Cecil Beaton, qui
excite bientôt la jalousie et l'esprit de compétition du
réalisateur George Cukor.

STILL FROM 'MY FAIR LADY' (1964)

Shaw's heroine, as recreated in the hit Broadway musical, was widely thought to 'belong' to Julie Andrews (not pictured) who sang and played the role wonderfully. Studio head Jack Warner insisted on Hepburn, who accepted the role on the condition that she sing for herself, without a "voice double." / Julie Andrews (nicht im Bild) schien die Rolle von Shaws Heldin für sich „gepachtet" zu haben, die sie in einem erfolgreichen Broadway-Musical wundervoll sang und spielte. Studioboss Jack Warner bestand hingegen auf Hepburn. Sie nahm die Rolle unter der Bedingung an,

selbst singen zu dürfen – ohne Stimmdouble. / L'héroïne de Shaw, telle qu'elle a été recréée dans la comédie musicale à succès jouée à Broadway, était pour nombre de gens définitivement « attachée » à Julie Andrews qui joua et chanta le rôle à merveille. Le directeur de studio Jack Warner insista pour qu'il revienne à Hepburn, qui était prête à l'accepter à condition qu'elle chante elle-même, sans « doublure de voix ».

STILL FROM 'MY FAIR LADY' (1964)

Despite long months of training, despite delivering a full score in her own voice that the film's music director, Andre Previn, fought hard to use, Cukor and Jack Warner elected to substitute a score sung by Marnie Nixon, a humiliating betrayal that probably cost Hepburn an Oscar nomination. / Trotz monatelanger Stimmübungen entschieden sich Cukor und Jack Warner für die Stimme von Marnie Nixon – der demütigende Verrat kostete Hepburn wahrscheinlich eine Oscar-Nominierung. / Malgré de longs mois de travail, Cukor et Jack Warner décidèrent pourtant de remplacer sa voix par celle de Marnie Nixon – une trahison humiliante qui a sans doute coûté à Hepburn une nomination aux Oscars.

WOMAN

★

DIE ERWACHSENE FRAU

UNE FEMME MÛRE

**STILL FROM 'HOW TO STEAL A MILLION'
(1966)**
Her clothes are so stylized in this caper that, in a rare
moment when she must dress as a cleaning lady to pull
off a heist, her partner and co-star Peter O'Toole
joked, "Give Givenchy the night off." / In diesem
Ganovenfilm waren ihre Kostüme stark stilisiert. Als
sie sich für ein Gaunerstück als Putzfrau verkleiden
musste, witzelte ihr Partner und Kollege Peter
O'Toole: „Givenchy hat heute mal frei." / Dans cette
comédie, ses vêtements étaient tellement chics que,
au bref moment où elle devait se déguiser en femme
de ménage pour déjouer un cambriolage, son
partenaire l'acteur Peter O'Toole lança en plaisantant :
« Dites à Givenchy qu'il peut disposer ce soir ! »

PAGE 152
PORTRAIT (1966)

ON THE SET OF 'HOW TO STEAL A MILLION' (1966)

Once again, and for a last time, reunited with her first great director, William Wyler (of 'Roman Holiday' and 'The Children's Hour'). / Erneut – und zum letzten Mal nach *Ein Herz und eine Krone* und *Infam* – spielte sie unter William Wyler, ihrem ersten großen Regisseur. / Une nouvelle et dernière collaboration avec le premier grand réalisateur à la diriger, William Wyler (*Vacances romaines* et *La Rumeur*).

156

STILL FROM 'TWO FOR THE ROAD' (1967)
A superbly honest, smartly structured study of a love
across decades, written by Frederic Raphael. / Die
wunderbar aufrichtige, geschickt aufgebaute Studie
einer Liebe über Jahrzehnte hinweg stammt aus der
Feder von Frederic Raphael. / Une étude
magnifiquement juste et menée avec finesse sur
l'amour à travers les âges, écrite par Frederic Raphael.

STILL FROM 'TWO FOR THE ROAD' (1967)
Hepburn plays a woman from age 20 to nearly 40 with
ease, in everyday clothes bought, as she put it "off the
peg." / Mühelos spielte Hepburn eine Frau zwischen
20 und fast 40 Jahren in Alltagskleidung, die nach
eigenen Worten „von der Stange" gekauft war. /
Hepburn joue vingt années de la vie d'une femme avec
aisance, vêtue de costumes quotidiens dénichés, selon
ses mots, « sur la corde à linge ».

STILL FROM 'TWO FOR THE ROAD' (1967)
Literally and metaphorically, Hepburn's Joanna is always the one who must "get out and push." / Im wörtlichen wie im übertragenen Sinn muss Hepburns Joanna immer „aussteigen und schieben". / Littéralement et métaphoriquement, la Joanna de Hepburn est toujours celle qui doit « descendre et pousser ».

STILL FROM 'TWO FOR THE ROAD' (1967)
Both are too sunburnt to touch, much less make love – yet they are determined. / Bei diesem Sonnenbrand können sich beide kaum anfassen, geschweige denn miteinander schlafen – aber ihrer Entschlossenheit tut das keinen Abbruch. / Tous deux ont trop de coups de soleil pour se toucher, encore moins faire l'amour – ils sont pourtant bien décidés.

"I've had so much more than I ever dreamed possible out of life - no great disappointments, or hopes that didn't work out: I didn't expect anything much, and because of that I'm the least bitter woman I know."
Audrey Hepburn

„Ich habe so viel mehr vom Leben bekommen, als ich mir je erträumt hatte - keine großen Enttäuschungen oder unerfüllte Hoffnungen. Ich habe nicht viel erwartet, und deshalb bin ich die am wenigsten verbitterte Frau, die ich kenne."
Audrey Hepburn

« La vie m'a donné tellement plus que tout ce dont j'ai pu rêver - aucune grave désillusion ni espoir déçu : je ne m'attendais à rien et c'est pourquoi je suis la femme la moins amère que je connaisse. »
Audrey Hepburn

STILL FROM 'TWO FOR THE ROAD' (1967)

The first indelible kiss which reveals to the pair that they are in love. Writer Frederic Raphael structures their love story into a large single journey across the south of France, catching this couple at different times in their life together: traveling as young lovers; as young marrieds on business; as a couple seeking renewal; as a pair of cool infidels pondering divorce; as a mature pair finding not merely passion, but abiding love, and life's meaning, in one another. / Der erste unvergessliche Kuss zeigt den beiden, dass sie sich lieben. Autor Frederic Raphael hat die Liebesgeschichte als eine einzige lange Reise durch Südfrankreich gestaltet, bei der man das Paar in verschiedenen Abschnitten ihres gemeinsamen Lebens sieht: als junges Liebespaar; als verheiratetes Paar auf Geschäftsreise, als Paar auf der Suche nach Erneuerung; als untreue Ehepartner, die die Scheidung erwägen; als reifes Paar, das im anderen nicht nur Leidenschaft findet, sondern dauerhafte Liebe und den Sinn des Lebens. / Ce premier baiser inoubliable leur révèle qu'ils sont amoureux. Le scénariste Frederic Raphael déroule leur histoire d'amour comme un voyage à travers le Sud de la France, région qu'ils parcourent à plusieurs époques de leur vie commune : amants juvéniles, jeunes mariés en voyage d'affaires, couple d'abord en quête d'un nouveau souffle, puis - infidèle et froid - envisageant le divorce et, enfin, la maturité venue, deux êtres qui dépassent la passion pour trouver l'un dans l'autre l'amour durable et le sens de la vie.

"*Audrey has a whim of iron.*"
Dory Previn

„*Audrey besitzt eine eiserne Laune.*"
Dory Previn

« *Audrey a une poigne de fer.* »
Dory Previn

STILL FROM 'TWO FOR THE ROAD' (1967)
Finney and Hepburn reveal an authentic intimacy,
tenderness and spontaneity in moment after moment.
It is no surprise that the actors had an affair during
filming. / Finney und Hepburn zeigen in jedem
Augenblick echte Intimität, Zärtlichkeit und
Spontaneität. Es überrascht kaum, dass die Schau-
spieler während der Dreharbeiten eine Affäre hatten. /
Finney et Hepburn exposent une authentique intimité,
une tendresse et une spontanéité de chaque instant.
Le fait que les deux acteurs aient eu une liaison
pendant le tournage ne surprend personne.

STILL FROM 'WAIT UNTIL DARK' (1967)
Hepburn prepared for this role as a recently blinded
woman with characteristic ferocity and attention to
detail. She spent weeks at Lighthouse, a rehabilitation
center for the blind. The studio wanted her to wear
dark glasses, or show some other overt indication of
her disability, like a scar, but she flatly refused. Instead
Hepburn created this heroine's sightlessness from the
inside out. / Mit charakteristischem Eifer und großer
Detailtreue bereitete sich Hepburn auf die Rolle einer
kurzlich erblindeten Frau vor. Sie verbrachte mehrere
Wochen im „Lighthouse", einem Reha-Zentrum für
Blinde. Das Studio wollte, dass sie eine Sonnenbrille
trug oder ihre Behinderung durch eine Narbe oder auf
andere Weise demonstrierte, aber sie lehnte dies
rundweg ab. Stattdessen spielte Hepburn die
Blindheit ihrer Figur von innen heraus. / Hepburn s'est
préparée à ce rôle de femme devenue aveugle avec
ardeur et méticulosité. Elle a passé des semaines au
Lighthouse, un centre de réinsertion pour aveugles.
Le studio voulait qu'elle porte des lunettes noires ou
quelque autre indice de son handicap, comme une
cicatrice, mais elle refusa catégoriquement. Hepburn
préférait exprimer la cécité de son héroïne par un jeu
qui venait de l'intérieur.

"I don't like the technique to show or even be there.
My hope was to do blindness from the inside out
and somehow convince the audience."
Audrey Hepburn

„Ich mag es nicht, wenn die Technik auffällt oder
auch nur vorhanden ist. Ich hatte gehofft, Blindheit
von innen heraus zu spielen und das Publikum
irgendwie zu überzeugen."
Audrey Hepburn

« Je n'aime pas que la technique soit visible, ou
même présente. Mon espoir était de jouer la cécité
de l'intérieur vers l'extérieur et de convaincre le
public, je ne sais comment. »
Audrey Hepburn

STILL FROM 'WAIT UNTIL DARK' (1967)
A fresh corpse (Samantha Jones) hanges in her
closet – and Susy (Hepburn) can sense something is
amiss, though she can't see it. / Die Leiche einer
soeben erwürgten Frau (Samantha Jones) hängt im
Kleiderschrank – Susy (Hepburn) spürt, dass hier
etwas nicht stimmt, auch wenn sie es nicht sehen
kann. / Le corps d'une femme étranglée (Samantha
Jones) a été suspendu dans son placard – et Susy
(Hepburn) sent que « quelque chose » ne va pas, sans
pourtant le voir.

STILL FROM 'WAIT UNTIL DARK' (1967)
Jack Weston (left) and Richard Crenna (silently brandishing a note reading 'husband'), are crooks attempting to manipulate Susy as evening falls. / Bei Nachtanbruch versuchen die Gauner Jack Weston (links) und Richard Crenna (der mit einem Zettel wedelt, auf dem das Wort „Ehemann" steht) Susy zu manipulieren. / Jack Weston (à gauche) et Richard Crenna (qui brandit silencieusement un billet sur lequel est écrit « mari ») sont des escrocs qui tentent de manipuler Susy le soir venu.

STILL FROM 'WAIT UNTIL DARK' (1967)
Roat (Alan Arkin) murdered the first girl with a long
knife he has nicknamed "Geraldine." Director Terence
Young wrests thrilling suspense from the confined
dark spaces of this single apartment, in what is nearly
real time. Hepburn's dawning awareness and Arkin's
seemingly unkillable menace drive the exceptional
climax. / Roat (Alan Arkin) ermordete das erste
Mädchen mit einem langen Messer, das er auf den
Namen „Geraldine" getauft hat. Fast in Echtzeit
erzeugt Regisseur Terence Young in den engen
dunklen Räumen der Wohnung nervenaufreibende
Spannung. Allmählich wird sich Susy der Gefahr
bewusst. Die Bedrohung durch Roat, der sie scheinbar
hilflos ausgeliefert ist, spitzt sich zu einem
außergewöhnlichen Höhepunkt zu. / Roat (Alan Arkin)
a tué la première fille avec un long couteau qu'il
surnomme « Geraldine ». Le réalisateur Terence Young
tire un suspense haletant des volumes sombres et
confinés de l'appartement, pour une intrigue qui se
déroule quasiment en temps réel jusqu'à l'apogée : la
prise de conscience d'Hepburn et la menace
visiblement inéluctable que représente Arkin.

PAGES 170/171
STILL FROM 'WAIT UNTIL DARK' (1967)
And here is the climax beyond the climax, when Roat,
whom we have seen to be dead, rises again by the
single cold light emanating from the apartment's
refrigerator. / Und hier der Höhepunkt nach dem
Höhepunkt. Der Zuschauer erkennt im Schein des
kalten Kühlschranklichts, wie der totgewähnte Roat
wieder aufsteht. / L'apogée de l'apogée : Roat, que
nous croyions mort, se relève et surgit dans la lumière
froide du frigo.

PORTRAIT FOR 'ROBIN AND MARIAN' (1976)
After a six year hiatus, Hepburn returned because she wanted to work with Sean Connery, and because she could have a grand romance playing a woman her own age. / Nach sechsjähriger Pause kehrte Hepburn auf die Leinwand zurück, weil sie mit Sean Connery arbeiten wollte und weil sie eine große Liebesgeschichte als Frau in ihrem Alter spielen konnte. / Après six ans d'absence, Hepburn revient à l'écran pour travailler avec Sean Connery et jouer une belle histoire d'amour dans le rôle d'une femme de son âge.

STILL FROM 'ROBIN AND MARIAN' (1976)
The carriage overturned by accident, with Hepburn in it, and director Richard Lester decided to work that into the plot. Hepburn was game, though she worried her heavy nun's gown would drown her like Ophelia. / Die Kutsche mit Hepburn stürzte unbeabsichtigt um, und Regisseur Richard Lester entschloss sich, den Unfall in die Handlung einzubauen. Hepburn spielte mit, obwohl sie Angst hatte, ihre schwere Ordenstracht würde sie wie Ophelia unter Wasser ziehen. / La charrette se renverse, avec Hepburn à l'intérieur, et le réalisateur Richard Lester décide d'intégrer l'incident à l'intrigue. Hepburn est partante, mais craint un instant que sa lourde robe de nonne ne la fasse sombrer comme Ophélie.

174

**STILL FROM 'SIDNEY SHELDON'S
BLOODLINE' (1979)**
Playing a younger woman in a mediocre melodrama.
Hepburn was frank about her reasons for accepting
the role - she was freshly divorced from her second
husband, and eager to salt away the million dollar fee
for her younger son, Luca. / In diesem mittelmäßigen
Melodram spielte sie wieder eine jüngere Frau.
Hepburn machte keinen Hehl daraus, weshalb sie
diese Rolle annahm: Sie hatte sich gerade von ihrem
zweiten Ehemann scheiden lassen und wollte die
Millionengage für ihren jüngeren Sohn Luca beiseite-
legen. / En femme plus jeune dans un mélo médiocre.
Hepburn explique franchement pourquoi elle a
accepté le rôle : elle venait de divorcer de son
deuxième époux et avait grand besoin du cachet d'un
million de dollars pour élever son fils cadet, Luca.

**PORTRAIT FOR 'SIDNEY SHELDON'S
BLOODLINE' (1979)**
Hepburn worked with designer Hubert de Givenchy
for the last time on this film. / In diesem Film arbeitete
Hepburn zum letzten Mal mit dem Modeschöpfer
Hubert de Givenchy zusammen. / Hepburn collabore
pour la dernière fois avec Hubert de Givenchy sur
ce film.

STILL FROM 'THEY ALL LAUGHED' (1982)

Director Peter Bogdanovich caught the earthy, bawdy side of Hepburn in this fine, underrated comedy, in which she and Ben Gazzara spark off each other. / In dieser hübschen, unterbewerteten Komödie, in der sich Hepburn und Ben Gazzara gegenseitig den Ball zuwarfen, fing Regisseur Peter Bogdanovich ihre derbe Seite hervorragend ein. / Le réalisateur Peter Bogdanovich joue du côté grivois et truculent de Hepburn dans cette charmante comédie sous-estimée où elle se livre avec Ben Gazzara à un jeu de répliques savoureux.

"Inspiration: That's the divine breath. It's what people count on. They reach for it, they pray for it. And quite often, just when they need it most, they get it: It's breathed into them. And now it's your turn to give it back."
Hap (Audrey Hepburn), 'Always' (1989)

„Inspiration: Das ist göttlicher Atem. Darauf verlassen sich die Menschen. Sie greifen danach, sie beten darum. Und ziemlich häufig, gerade wenn sie sie am nötigsten brauchen, bekommen sie sie: Sie wird ihnen eingehaucht. Und jetzt sind Sie an der Reihe, sie zurückzugeben."
Hap (Audrey Hepburn), Always – Der Feuerengel von Montana (1989)

STILL FROM 'ALWAYS' (1989)
Steven Spielberg is, as scholar Joseph McBride has observed, the last great director to emerge from the old studio system. How fitting that Hepburn should end her career under his direction – and playing an angel, at that, opposite Richard Dreyfuss. / Nach Aussage des Filmkenners Joseph McBride ist Steven Spielberg der letzte große Regisseur, der aus dem alten Studiosystem hervorging. So passte es auch gut, dass Hepburn ihre Karriere unter seiner Regie beendete – noch dazu als Engel an der Seite von Richard Dreyfuss. / Steven Spielberg est, comme l'a observé Joseph McBride, le dernier grand réalisateur à émerger du vieux système des studios. Quel beau hasard qu'Audrey Hepburn ait achevé sa carrière sous sa direction – et dans le rôle d'un ange, face à Richard Dreyfuss !

« L'inspiration, c'est le souffle divin. C'est ce sur quoi les gens comptent. Ils la recherchent, prient pour qu'elle les touche. Et assez souvent, au moment où ils en ont le plus besoin, ils la reçoivent : elle s'insuffle en eux. Et maintenant, c'est à vous de la restituer. »
Hap (Audrey Hepburn), *Always – Pour toujours* (1989)

3

CHRONOLOGY

CHRONOLOGIE

CHRONOLOGIE

1929 Audrey Kathleen Hepburn is born on 4 May in Brussels, Belgium.

1931–1935 The family lives in England, where her banker father is active in the British Fascist movement led by Oswald Mosley. Her father walks out on the family.

1936–1939 Commutes between her mother's family estate in Arnhem, Holland, and London, where her father enrolls her in a ballet school. As war breaks out in September 1939, her mother gets exclusive custody of Audrey. It will be another 20 years before she sets eyes on her father again.

1940 On 17 May performs as a chorus ballerina with Margot Fonteyn in a touring production of Frederick Ashton's *Horoscope*. That night the Nazi invasion commences 12 miles away.

1941–1945 Her mother, renouncing her former husband's fascist sympathies, becomes active in the Dutch resistance. Separated from her mother for over a month, Audrey hides in a barn and starves, dodging the Nazi roundups. Audrey nearly dies of jaundice.

1946–1947 An attack of edema temporarily wrecks her ankles. She recovers (thanks to food packages from the United Nations Relief Fund, the forerunner of UNICEF) but her ballet career is cut short because she is too tall.

1948 After playing the tiny role of an airline hostess in her first film, *Dutch in 7 Lessons*, Audrey and her mother leave Holland and move to London.

1951 Plays supporting roles for Ealing studios.

1952 Colette, author of the novel *Gigi*, notices Audrey on the set of *We Go to Monte Carlo* (1952), and proclaims her an ideal Gigi for Broadway – and a star is born.

1953 Wins an Academy Award for *Roman Holiday* (1953), becomes world famous and enjoys a major film career that continues unabated until she voluntarily retires after *Wait Until Dark* (1967). On *Sabrina* (1954), she has a passionate affair with William Holden and begins a lifelong collaboration with fashion designer Hubert de Givenchy.

1954 On 25 September marries her co-star from the play *Ondine* (1954), actor-director Mel Ferrer. Her first pregnancy ends in a miscarriage.

1959 Suffers her second miscarriage when thrown from a horse during the filming of *The Unforgiven* (1960). Privately reunites with her father, now a pensioner in Dublin. She sees to his material comforts for the rest of his life. Becomes pregnant and stops acting to protect the baby.

1960 Birth of her son Sean Ferrer on 7 July.

1964–1965 Has an affair with Albert Finney while making *Two for the Road* (1966).

1968–1969 The marriage to Mel Ferrer, which had disintegrated in the early 1960s, ends in divorce. Audrey marries Andrea Dotti, and retires from public life.

1970 Birth of Luca Dotti, her second son.

1976–1979 Returns to the public eye with *Robin and Marian* (1976), and earns a cool million starring in a dud, *Sydney Sheldon's Bloodline* (1977). Divorces Andrea Dotti in 1979.

1980–1989 Although she continues to act, Audrey's primary focus is on her two sons, on making a life with Robert Wolders in Tolochenaz, Switzerland, and philanthropic work. In 1989 she becomes the global Ambassador for UNICEF.

1992 Tours Somalia in her role as goodwill ambassador between 20-24 September. Although toughened by her own childhood and frequent trips for UNICEF, the teeming masses of dying and starved children, especially in Mogadishu, devastate her spiritually and physically. In November, she is diagnosed with colon cancer in Los Angeles, and surgery is unsuccessful.

1993 On 20 January, Audrey Hepburn dies at home in Tolochenaz.

PAGE 178
PORTRAIT (1954)
"I'm not stacked like Sophia Loren or Gina Lollobrigida, but I don't need a bedroom to prove my womanliness." / „Ich habe nicht viel Holz vor der Hütte wie Sophia Loren oder Gina Lollobrigida, aber ich brauche kein Schlafzimmer, um zu beweisen, dass ich eine Frau bin."/ « Je ne suis pas carrossée comme Sophia Loren ou Gina Lollobrigida, mais je n'ai pas besoin d'une chambre pour prouver ma féminité. »

PORTRAIT FOR 'SABRINA' (1954)
"The first thing I saw when I came to America was The Statue of Liberty. The second - [photographer] Richard Avedon." / „Als Erstes sah ich in Amerika die Freiheitsstatue, als Zweites - [den Fotografen] Richard Avedon." / « La première chose que j'ai vue en arrivant en Amérique, c'est la statue de la Liberté. La deuxième, c'est [le photographe] Richard Avedon. »

CHRONOLOGIE

1929 Audrey Kathleen Hepburn wird am 4. Mai in der belgischen Hauptstadt Brüssel geboren.

1931–1935 Die Familie lebt in England. Der Vater, ein Bankier, engagiert sich in der britischen Faschistenbewegung unter der Führung von Oswald Mosley und verlässt seine Familie.

1936–1939 Sie pendelt zwischen dem Familiensitz ihrer Mutter in Arnheim (Niederlande) und London, wo ihr Vater sie in einer Ballettschule anmeldet. Als im September 1939 der Krieg ausbricht, erhält ihre Mutter das alleinige Sorgerecht für Audrey. Erst 20 Jahre später sieht sie ihren Vater wieder.

1940 Am 17. Mai tritt sie als Ballerina in einer Tanzgruppe unter Margot Fonteyn in einer Tourneeaufführung von Frederick Ashtons *Horoscope* auf. Nur 19 km entfernt fällt die Wehrmacht in die Niederlande ein.

1941–1945 Die Mutter engagiert sich im niederländischen Widerstand. Audrey wird über einen Monat lang von ihrer Mutter getrennt. Sie stirbt beinahe an Gelbsucht.

1946–1947 Sie erkrankt an Wassersucht und kann vorübergehend nicht mehr laufen. Dank der Nahrungspakete des United Nations Relief Fund erholt sie sich wieder. Ihre Ballettlaufbahn kann sie aufgrund ihrer Körpergröße aber nicht fortsetzen.

1948 Nachdem sie in ihrem ersten Film *Nederlands in 7 lessen* die winzige Rolle einer Flugbegleiterin gespielt hat, verlässt sie mit ihrer Mutter die Niederlande und zieht nach London.

1951 Sie spielt Nebenrollen für die Ealing-Studios

1952 Colette, die Verfasserin des Romans *Gigi*, bemerkt Audrey bei den Dreharbeiten zu *Musik in Monte Carlo* (1952) und erklärt sie zur perfekten Gigi für den Broadway – damit ist ein neuer Star geboren.

1953 Sie gewinnt den Oscar für *Ein Herz und eine Krone* (1953), wird weltberühmt. Nach *Warte, bis es dunkel ist* (1967) zieht sie sich vorerst aus dem Filmgeschäft zurück. Bei den Dreharbeiten für *Sabrina* (1954) lässt sie sich auf eine leidenschaftliche Affäre mit ihrem Kollegen William Holden ein und beginnt die lebenslange Zusammenarbeit mit dem Modeschöpfer Hubert de Givenchy.

1954 Am 25. September heiratet sie den Schauspieler und Regisseur Mel Ferrer, mit dem sie in dem Stück *Ondine* (1954) auf der Bühne stand. Ihre erste Schwangerschaft endet mit einer Fehlgeburt.

1959 Erlebt eine zweite Fehlgeburt, als sie während der Dreharbeiten zu *Denen man nicht vergibt* (1960) vom Pferd stürzt. Sie sieht erstmals ihren Vater wieder, der inzwischen als Rentner in Dublin lebt. Bis zu seinem Lebensende sorgt sie für seinen Unterhalt. Sie wird wieder schwanger und unterbricht das Drehen, um das Kind nicht zu gefährden.

1960 Am 7. Juli kommt ihr erster Sohn Sean Ferrer zur Welt.

1964–1965 Während der Dreharbeiten zu *Zwei auf gleichem Weg* (1966) hat sie eine Affäre mit Albert Finney.

1968–1969 Die Ehe mit Mel Ferrer, die bereits Anfang der sechziger Jahre zerbrochen war, wird geschieden. Audrey heiratet Andrea Dotti und zieht sich aus der Öffentlichkeit zurück.

1970 Ihr zweiter Sohn Luca Dotti kommt zur Welt.

1976–1979 Sie kehrt mit *Robin and Marian* (*Robin und Marian*, 1976) auf die Leinwand zurück und kassiert eine Millionengage für ihre Hauptrolle in dem Flop *Blutspur* (1977). Im Jahre 1979 lässt sie sich von Andrea Dotti scheiden.

1980–1989 Obwohl Audrey weiterhin Filme dreht, gilt ihre Aufmerksamkeit in erster Linie ihrer Privatsphäre und ihrem philanthropischen Engagement. Im Jahre 1989 wird sie UNICEF-Botschafterin.

1992 Reist vom 20. bis 24. September durch Somalia. Die vielen hungernden und sterbenden Kinder, insbesondere in Mogadischu, nehmen sie körperlich und seelisch stark mit. Im November stellt man in Los Angeles bei ihr Darmkrebs fest, der anschließende Eingriff ist aber erfolglos.

1993 Am 20. Januar stirbt Audrey Hepburn in ihrem Haus in Tolochenaz.

PORTRAIT (1954)
"I depend on Givenchy in the same way that American women depend on their psychiatrists." / „Ich verlasse mich in der gleichen Weise auf Givenchy, wie sich Amerikanerinnen auf ihre Psychiater verlassen." / « J'ai besoin de Givenchy de la même manière que les femmes américaines ont besoin de leur psychiatre. »

CHRONOLOGIE

1929 Audrey Kathleen Hepburn voit le jour le 4 mai à Bruxelles, en Belgique.

1931–1935 La famille vit en Angleterre, où son père, banquier, est un membre actif du parti fasciste britannique mené par Oswald Mosley. Son père quitte la famille.

1936–1939 Partage son temps entre la maison familiale de sa mère à Arnhem, en Hollande, et Londres, où son père l'a fait entrer dans une école de danse. Lorsque la guerre éclate en septembre 1939, sa mère obtient la garde exclusive d'Audrey. Elle attendra 20 ans avant de revoir son père.

1940 Le 17 mai, elle figure parmi la troupe qui danse aux côtés de Margot Fonteyn au cours d'une tournée de *Horoscope* de Frederick Ashton. Cette nuit-là, l'invasion nazie commence, à une vingtaine de kilomètres.

1941–1945 Sa mère, qui rejette les sympathies fascistes de son ex-mari, devient un membre actif de la résistance hollandaise. Séparée d'elle pendant plus d'un mois, Audrey se terre dans une grange pour échapper aux rafles nazies. Elle souffre de la faim et succombe presque à une jaunisse.

1946–1947 Une poussée d'œdème lui endommage les chevilles. Elle guérit (grâce aux colis de ravitaillement fournis par le fonds d'aide des Nations Unies) mais sa carrière de danseuse est interrompue : elle est devenue trop grande.

1948 Après un petit rôle d'hôtesse de l'air dans son premier film, *Le Hollandais en 7 leçons*, Audrey et sa mère quittent la Hollande pour Londres.

1951 Joue des seconds rôles pour les studios Ealing.

1952 Colette remarque Audrey sur le plateau de *Nous irons à Monte Carlo* (1952) et décrète qu'elle est la « Gigi » qu'il faut pour Broadway. Une étoile est née.

AUDREY HEPBURN

"I'm half Irish, half Dutch, and I was born in Belgium. If I was a dog I'd be a hell of a mess." / „Ich bin halb irischer, halb niederländischer Abstammung, und ich wurde in Belgien geboren. Als Hund wäre ich eine ganz schöne Promenadenmischung."/ « Je suis moitié Irlandaise, moitié Hollandaise et je suis née en Belgique. Si j'étais un chien, je ne ressemblerais à rien. »

1953 Remporte un oscar pour *Vacances romaines* (1953), devient mondialement célèbre et profite d'une carrière qui se poursuit avec la même intensité jusqu'à ce qu'elle se retire volontairement des projecteurs après *Seule dans la nuit* (1967). Sur le tournage de *Sabrina* (1954), elle vit une aventure fougueuse avec William Holden et débute sa longue collaboration avec Hubert de Givenchy.

1954 Le 25 septembre, elle épouse son partenaire de la pièce *Ondine* (1954), l'acteur et réalisateur Mel Ferrer. Enceinte, elle fait une fausse couche.

1959 Subit sa deuxième fausse couche en tombant de cheval sur le tournage du *Vent de la plaine* (1960). Dans le privé, elle retrouve son père, désormais retraité à Dublin. Elle veille à son confort matériel jusqu'à sa mort. Retombe enceinte et arrête de jouer pour protéger ce bébé.

1960 Naissance de son fils Sean Ferrer le 7 juillet.

1964–1965 A une aventure avec Albert Finney sur le tournage de *Voyage à deux* (1966).

1968–1969 Son mariage avec Mel Ferrer, qui a implosé au début des années 1960, se solde par un divorce. Audrey épouse Andrea Dotti et se retire de la vie publique.

1970 Naissance de Luca Dotti, son second fils.

1976–1979 Retourne devant la caméra pour *La Rose et la Flèche* (1976) et empoche une coquette somme pour le premier rôle dans le très raté *Liés par le sang* de Sydney Sheldon (1977). Divorce d'Andrea Dotti en 1979.

1980–1989 Bien qu'elle continue à jouer, Audrey se concentre surtout sur ses deux films, sur sa nouvelle vie amoureuse avec Robert Wolders à Tolochenaz, en Suisse, et sur ses missions philanthropiques. En 1989, elle devient Ambassadrice itinérante de l'UNICEF.

1992 Se rend en Somalie en tant qu'ambassadrice de l'UNICEF du 20 au 24 septembre. Les hordes d'enfants affamés et agonisants, en particulier à Mogadiscio, la dévastent psychologiquement et physiquement. En novembre, les médecins diagnostiquent un cancer du colon incurable.

1993 Le 20 janvier, Audrey Hepburn rend l'âme à son domicile de Tolochenaz.

4

FILMOGRAPHY

★

FILMOGRAFIE

FILMOGRAPHIE

RLD'S GREATEST NOVEL...translated into nearly every language, now receives its most magnificent translation of all...into the universal language of the

Just as no greater novel has ever been written, no motion picture up to this time has ever spread such a limitless canvas of appeal to ticket-buyers of all ages. In "War and Peace" are dramatized a young man's first taste of battle, a young girl's first taste of love, a young mind's first taste of ideas, a man's first taste of old age. Here truly is the complete and thrilling panorama of the human heart to entice the maximum audience everywhere.

Tolstoy's immortal novel has been deemed too enor
s to be encompassed in a motion picture. This miracle
now been achieved by Paramount . . . as this world-
aimed masterpiece, in all its power, is at last con
ed in 3 hours and 28 minutes of absorbing boxoffice
ertainment. Your patrons will wish there was more!

Dutch in 7 Lessons/Nederlands in 7 lessen/Le Hollandais en 7 leçons (1948)

One Wild Oat/One Wild Oat/Une avoine sauvage (1951)

Laughter in Paradise/Wer zuletzt lacht/Rires au paradis (1951)

Young Wives Tale/Mit Küchenbenutzung/Histoire de jeunes femmes (1951)

The Lavender Hill Mob/Einmal Millionär sein/ De l'or en barre (1951)

The Secret People/Die Verblendeten/Secret People (1952)

We Go to Monte Carlo (aka Monte Carlo Baby/ Baby Beats the Band)/Musik in Monte Carlo/ Nous irons à Monte Carlo (1952)

Roman Holiday/Ein Herz und eine Krone/ Vacances romaines (1953)

Sabrina (1954)

War and Peace/Krieg und Frieden/Guerre et Paix (1956)

Funny Face/Ein süßer Fratz/Drôle de frimousse (1957)

Love in the Afternoon (aka Ariane)/Ariane - Liebe am Nachmittag/Ariane (1957)

Green Mansions/Green Mansions/Vertes demeures (1959)

The Nun's Story/Geschichte einer Nonne/Au risque de se perdre (1959)

The Unforgiven/Denen man nicht vergibt/Le Vent de la plaine (1960)

Breakfast at Tiffany's/Frühstück bei Tiffany/ Diamants sur canapé (1961)

PAGE 186
PORTRAIT FOR 'BREAKFAST AT TIFFANY'S'
(1961)

The Children's Hour (aka *The Loudest Whisper*)/
Infam/La Rumeur (1962)

Charade (1963)

*Paris When It Sizzles/Zusammen in Paris/Deux
têtes folles* (1964)

My Fair Lady (1964)

*How to Steal a Million/Wie klaut man eine
Million?/Comment voler un million de dollars*
(1966)

*Two for the Road/Zwei auf gleichem Weg/Voyage
à deux* (1967)

*Wait Until Dark/Warte, bis es dunkel ist (a. Warte,
bis es dunkel wird)/Seule dans la nuit* (1967)

*Robin and Marian/Robin und Marian/La Rose et
la Flèche* (1976)

*Sidney Sheldon's Bloodline/Blutspur/Liés par le
sang* (1979)

*They All Laughed/Sie haben alle gelacht/Et tout
le monde riait* (1982)

*Always/Always – Der Feuerengel von
Montana/Always – Pour toujours* (1989)

Television/Fernsehen/Télévision

Mayerling (1959)

*Love Among Thieves/Flashpoint Mexico/Love
Among Thieves* (1987)

Theater/Theater/Théâtre

Gigi (1951)

Ondine (1954)

STILL FROM 'CHARADE' (1963)
A fan once gushed, "You have the most beautiful eyes in the world." She would have none of it: "The most beautiful eye make-up, maybe." / Ein Fan schwärmte einmal: „Sie haben die schönsten Augen der Welt." Das wollte sie nicht gelten lassen: „Vielleicht das schönste Augen-Make-up."/ Un admirateur s'extasia un jour : « Vous avez les plus beaux yeux du monde ». Elle refusa ce compliment : « Disons, peut-être le plus beau maquillage. »

BIBLIOGRAPHY

Crowe, Cameron: *Conversations with Wilder.* Knopf, 1999.

Ferrer, Sean Hepburn: *Audrey Hepburn, an elegant spirit.* Atria Books, 2003.

Higham, Charles: *Audrey Hepburn.* Macmillan, 1984.

Huston, John: *An Open Book.* Knopf, 1980.

Morely, Sheridan: *Audrey Hepburn, a celebration.* Pavilion Books, 1993.

Sembach, Klaus-Jürgen, translated by Michael Robertson: *Adieu, Audrey.* Schirmer Art Books, 1993.

Stevens, Jr., George: *Conversations with the Great Filmmakers of Hollywood's Golden Age.* Knopf, 2006.

Thomson, David: *A Biographical Dictionary of Film (third edition).* Knopf, 1993.

Walker, Alexander: *Audrey, Her Real Story.* St. Martin's Press, 1994.

Willoughby, Bob: *Audrey, an intimate collection.* Vision On, 2002.

Wood, Tom: *The Bright Side of Billy Wilder, Primarily.* Doubleday, 1970.

Woodward, Ian: *Audrey Hepburn.* St. Martin's Press, 1984.

IMPRINT

© 2006 TASCHEN GmbH
Hohenzollernring 53, D-50672 Köln
www.taschen.com

Editor/Picture Research/Layout: Paul Duncan/Wordsmith Solutions
Editorial Coordination: Martin Holz, Cologne
Production Coordination: Nadia Najm and Horst Neuzner, Cologne
German translation: Thomas J. Kinne, Nauheim
French translation: Alice Petillot, Paris
Multilingual production: www.arnaudbriand.com, Paris
Typeface Design: Sense/Net, Andy Disl and Birgit Reber, Cologne

Printed in Italy
ISBN-13: 978-3-8228-2001-8
ISBN-10: 3-8228-2001-6

To stay informed about upcoming TASCHEN titles, please request our magazine at www.taschen.com/magazine or write to TASCHEN, Hohenzollernring 53, D-50672 Cologne, Germany, contact@taschen.com, Fax: +49-221-254919. We will be happy to send you a free copy of our magazine which is filled with information about all of our books.

All the photos in this book, except for those listed below, were supplied by The Kobal Collection.

The Azcona-Serrano Collection: pp. 70, 72, 73, 74, 75

ENDPAPERS/VORSATZ/PAGES DE GARDE
PORTRAITS FOR 'BREAKFAST AT TIFFANY'S' (1961)

PAGES 2/3
STILL FROM 'LOVE IN THE AFTERNOON' (1957)

PAGE 4
PORTRAIT FOR 'FUNNY FACE' (1957)

PAGE 6
PORTRAIT

PAGES 8/9
PORTRAIT FOR 'FUNNY FACE' (1957)